GOD'S *Transforming* SPIRIT: BLACK CHURCH RENEWAL

Preston Robert Washington

Judson Press® Valley Forge

GOD'S TRANSFORMING SPIRIT: BLACK CHURCH RENEWAL

Copyright © 1988
Judson Press, Valley Forge, PA 19482–0851
Second Printing, 1989

The Scripture quotations in this book are taken from the Revised Standard Version of the Bible copyrighted 1946, 1952 © 1971, 1973 by the Division of Christian Education of the National Council of the Churches of Christ in the U.S.A., and used by permission. Other Scriptures are taken from *The Holy Bible,* King James Version; *Good News Bible,* the Bible in Today's English Version, Copyright © American Bible Society, 1976. Used by permission; and *The Living Bible,* Tyndale House Publishers, Wheaton, Ill. Used by permission.

LIBRARY OF CONGRESS
Library of Congress Cataloging-in-Publication Data

Washington, Preston Robert.
   God's transforming spirit : Black church renewal / by Preston
Robert Washington.
     p. cm.
   Bibliography: p.
   ISBN 0–8170–1129–3 :
   1. Church renewal. 2. Memorial Baptist Church (Harlem, New York,
N.Y.) 3. Harlem (New York, N.Y.)—Church history. I. Title.
BV600.2.W345 1988
250'.8996073—dc19
                                                     88–21580
                                                          CIP

The name JUDSON PRESS is registered as a trademark in the U.S. Patent Office.
Printed in the U.S.A.

THIS BOOK IS DEDICATED TO

the black matriarchs of faith
who helped me to fall in love
with God's continuing creation—
the church of Jesus Christ.

They are Eva Brown, great-grandmother;
Nancy Washington, grandmother; Effitee Mae Moore,
godmother; Susan Battle, special friend;
who are now departed; and
LuLu DeCasseres, grandmother; Willette Washington,
mother; Elizabeth, Mildred, and Mary Moore,
mother surrogates; and Helen Messer Ullah,
mother-in-law.

Contents

Foreword

This book is written as a response to a personal challenge. I am keenly aware of the lack of resources on the market for black urban congregations seeking renewal and growth. Therefore, it was my decision in 1979 to begin documenting some of the exciting events, programs, and plans that marked my ministerial journey, most specifically as an urban pastor but also as a denominational executive and a facilitator in church planning, renewal, and development. This book did not fall ready-made from the skies, however. I first tried my hand at writing an initial book[1] on church outreach and growth from a biblical and theological perspective, but only then did I realize that I had not sufficiently lifted up some of the flesh-and-blood learnings from my experiences in the trenches. Anton Boisen speaks of "the living human document" as the most forgotten source of theology.[2] It became increasingly clear to me that a forgotten side of church renewal, growth, and development was, in addition to program development, the analysis of the *place* as well as the *people* who will make change possible. As a pastor of a coming-alive church, I have intentionally taken the route and the risk of telling one congregation's story of growth and development. Hopefully, you the reader will peruse this work with an eye toward your own ministry choices and challenges.

This book is written for pastors, lay members, denominational executives, seminary students and professors, social science community development activists, and anyone else who shares the belief that the local church is one crucial instrument for bringing about justice, reconciliation, empowerment, and peace, especially to a world that is becoming increasingly urbanized and stratified by race, class, age, and gender differences.

The ways to renewal and growth proposed in these pages certainly are not the only methods and strategies possible for churches in desperate need of transformation. In telling our renewal story, perhaps there will be some hints, some helps, some aha's! that will generate your own creative thinking about how our Shalom-bringing God might impact your church, community, seminary, denomination, or life to the end that we might all become more faithful to the call of God in this contemporary age.

This story is a *montage*. Pieces of it are captured in the form of documents that I have written to motivate the membership to share in the goal of renewal and growth. Some material represents journal notes and remembrances from the file of my mind. Much more of it is selected from the minutes, meeting notes, and congregational training materials that have been collected from 1976 to 1987 at the Memorial Baptist Church, Inc. of Harlem, New York.

While serving as pastor of Memorial Church, I also was blessed with the opportunity to work as an associate executive minister of American Baptist Churches of Metropolitan New York from 1979 to 1983. Therefore, all the insights here are not the exclusive property of our church. Memorial Church collectively, and I personally, owe an incredible debt to the American Baptist Churches (ABC) of Metropolitan New York and to my renewal ministry colleagues the Reverends Carl E. Flemister, Donald M. Morlan, Allen Hinand, and administrative board members. Through the invaluable training and work with the more than 187 local ABC Metro churches, I discovered how essential it is to participate in a collegium of denominational staff, pastors, and laity where theology is made relevant, reverent, and real. As a denominational executive and pastor, such exposure to the stimulating discussions related to church growth, renewal, and development strengthened my commitment to the church in the city.

Writing a book about *any* group of people, many of whom are yet breathing, is a risky business. Once in-house secrets are revealed, it inevitably changes the dynamics within that organization. It is not my intention to air problems or in any way exploit my congregation. The prayerful hope I now live with, after more than a decade in pastoral ministry in a transforming/renewing congregation, is that Memorial's heroic and courageous struggle to become a beacon light in Central Harlem will be an inspiration to many other pastors, lay leaders, denominational executives, and congregations who find themselves in the wilderness of spiritual malaise and despair.

The story of Memorial Baptist Church of Harlem is just one small example of a larger enterprise involving coming-alive congregations across the nation, and, indeed, around the world. What is highlighted here are some of the ways in which God's transforming Spirit is at work in one church in one community.

I would like to thank personally the men and women of the official board and members of the Memorial Church for their willingness to mentor me and for allowing me the privilege of serving them as their pastor. This book would not have been possible without their special trust and tempering.

Assistant to the pastor Reverend Mariah Ann Britton, as well as my wife, Maria Ullah, and our son, Jamel-Tahir, have provided listening ears and remarkable support. Elizabeth Brown, Gloria Denise Wright, and James Dudley gave important assistance in the typing/word processing preparation of the original draft.

Minister Donna Lyn Smith-Taylor, my administrative assistant, is to be credited for lending invaluable technical expertise in the preparation of this present manuscript. Reverend Marsha Woodard gave important editorial shape and coherency to this study.

This has been a collective effort. Only the mistakes are my own.

Liberated because of Calvary,

Preston Robert Washington
Central Harlem, 1988

Preface

Journal and Journey

There is much talk these days about church growth, church renewal, and church development, and depending upon the author and particular philosophy, these terms are used to signify different things. However, the thrust of this book focuses on the widespread need for church and congregational renewal.[1] The *Merriam-Webster Dictionary* defined the word "renew": "To make or become new, fresh or strong again, to restore to existence, recreate, revive . . . and replace."[2]

Like a sailboat at sea, the contemporary church is often drifting without benefit of wind to push it or a captain to direct it. The fact is that both lay members and professional clergy of late have expressed deep concern for the contemporary church and its all-too-frequent inability to generate internal energy to renew itself and to effectively transform the world.[3]

True, our times are critical indeed. Congregational and community renewal must somehow take place in the midst of abounding media religions, fundamentalist hypes, cultist movements, nominal fads, and religious smoke screens for conservative political dogma. Today's man or woman of faith must seek to hear the voice of God, to use Gene Bartlett's idea, amidst a "cacophony of voices" all peddling their particular wares to gain power, prestige, and prominence among unsuspecting men and women.[4] The confusion of contemporary clergy and laity on a personal level is more often than not reflective of an institutional confusion as well. The church as an institution is in trouble. Many a congregation needs to be renewed, revived, and rekindled. It needs to be made strong and fresh again. Sometimes a congregation (we trust not often) needs to be replaced if its renewal and its community transformation possibilities are not realized over time.

Every book to some degree reflects the particular cultural standing of the author. My perspective is essentially black urban Baptist. I attended black Baptist and Pentecostal churches during my childhood years and hence reflect in my ministry a sense of my Afro-American spiritual roots. But I pray that I am not parochial. I grew up in East Harlem (El Barrio), where lessons abound for the need to understand different ethnic groups—Puerto Ricans, Italians, Jews, whites; a host of assorted black people: Southerners, West Indians, urban blacks—all of whom represented a slice of life that made the pie of our community what it was. I suspect that this early multiethnic exposure prepared me in many ways to minister to a rich and varied constituency in metropolitan New York.

As a teenage preacher (I started at age thirteen) who loved the enthusiasm and warmth of our storefront church, I tried desperately to personally work out, as early as I could, a liveable theology that connected what I experienced on the pavements to the happenings in the pew and vice-versa. The times of my growing up put a stamp on me and my sermons. Black national luminaries such as Malcolm X; Lerone Bennett; Martin Luther King, Jr.; Stokely Carmichael; Gwendolyn Brooks; James Cone; and the pastor of my youth, Rev. Jacob Hillery (among others); all influenced my life in countless ways.

Unfortunately, my teenage attempt at practical theology proved abortive at first. My childhood minister was not impressed with my tentative spiritual discoveries. So like a prodigal son, I journeyed to college, seminary, Africa, Europe, the Caribbean, and several urban communities in the United States in search of an integrative experience to understand how, indeed, I could be a relevant Christian and minister in the midst of the 1960s. My personal search gave me some insights into the church and how it can respond to its times and come alive.

My childhood storefront church died. It could not make the difficult adjustment to the realities of the late twentieth century. The leadership was not always able to deal with kids on drugs, teenage pregnancies, school and family crises, housing shortages, and the deteriorated socioeconomic and spiritual landscape of the inner city. For them it became more and more difficult to speak a creative word for the Lord in the desolate terrain where they found themselves.

Other congregations also have become casualties in these times. Perhaps many of them could not hold out against the outer storms of social, economic, political, cultural, and spiritual change or they simply rotted and decayed internally. Still others, in their closing, could celebrate a triumphant pattern of ministry as their membership scattered or merged with other congregations.

The long and short of this book is that renewal comes about when

1. The pastor and people in the congregation are mutually nurtured and affirmed
2. The church becomes intentional about it
3. The congregation, or significant parts of it, sees a need for revitalizing itself
4. The congregation seeks to be relevant in relation to its community and the world.

The congregation takes a serious look at itself in relation to what it understands as God's intention for it and what it should do in relation to the needs of the community and the worldwide reality. Many congregations have lost (if they ever had) the *zeal* to be a prophetic and explosive power as witnesses in their communities and God's world. That is why the title of this book is *God's Transforming Spirit: Black Church Renewal.* It is not a novel concept, but in every generation the church is in need of a *spiritual radicalization.* It needs new zeal, new purpose, new self-image, new leadership. I offer this reflective action plan to laypersons, clergy, seminarians, and administrative and denominational executives who sense the need for renewal in their congregations and are willing to be intentional about opening themselves to the Spirit's surprises and possibilities.

This book, then, is both journal and journey. It is a reflective study of my unfolding ministry as an urban pastor. It also is a story of how one black congregation has caught the renewal spirit and grown numerically and qualitatively as well.

In so many ways the work outlined here is not complete. This is merely a sketch of some of the learnings which have blessed our witness in *one* urban arena where the Good News struggles to be heard and lived.

As I seek to interpret our discoveries as a renewing congregation, it is admitted that much of what we say now is *after* the fact; after we have experimented and sometimes failed or accidentally found procedures and strategies that worked wonders for us.

The overall goal of this book is to demonstrate that church renewal is not accomplished through the expertise of experts only, but must be a partnership between laity, pastors, denominational leaders, and the community where the congregation finds itself. Church renewal, then, is a partnership ministry, a collaborative effort, a shared happening.

The basic movement of this journal-journey is as follows: In Chapter 1 I focus on the tensions and struggles inherent in a first-time pastorate. The optimistic seminarian or minister who is called to a church may find out that all may not be well in the congregation. Usually one discovers this reality after the so-called "honeymoon" between pulpit and pew has ended. The goal of Chapter 1 is to provide some practical guidelines in developing a pastoral prayer discipline accompanied by an increasing awareness that change is a *process* that must be "owned" by the pew before it can become an exciting, healthy, and vital reality in congregational life.

In Chapter 2 I expand the idea of personal pastoral prayer to include churchwide program development. It is my contention that prayer is "the royal road" to church renewal, because it helps a congregation to take seriously the tensions, pains, crises, and joys within the lives of the membership as well as in the minister's own family and personal life. The objective of this chapter is to determine how a congregation can develop maximum opportunities for prayer development—especially for new believers, as well as develop leaders for prayer ministries within a church.

The question that concerns a recovering and renewing congregation is, How do we get started? In Chapter 3 I analyze some of the ways one church community began to intentionally focus on renewal concerns. It may be a relief to some leaders, both lay and clergy, that although renewal must *ultimately* include a large portion of the congregation, in its initial development a small "leaven" group trained in Bible study, prayer discipline, communication skills, and the planning process can begin to light the fires of congregational change. The goal of a renewing congregation is to develop a vision. Some practical suggestions are included to get you and/or your church to begin to think about ways to initiate the vision process.

In Chapters 4 and 5, I outline two models of ministry in our local congregation: "inreach" and "outreach" strategies. These are lifted up because they helped us *prioritize* our ministry vision goals, or put another way, to scratch people where they itch. What good is it to enlist new members in the church if there is no intentional design to train them for ministry, let alone keep them? "Revolving-Door Christians" characterize many a church community. In Chapter 4 I include some practical and theological guides for not only keeping new members, but hopefully growing and maturing them for kingdom work as well.

Chapter 5 takes a different tack. It outlines some practical ways a congregation can become involved in mission right in its own community. Some sociological perspectives are included here to help renewal leaders recognize that the congregation must come to identify, plan with, and/or confront some of the social, political, and economic systems that impact upon that congregation and its community. Renewal is not just what goes on inside the four walls of the church building. As transformation becomes contagious it tends to raise the consciousness of next-door neighbors in the community as much as it does the folk in the church. Renewal also helps a congregation overcome its sense of isolation and powerlessness as it begins to build coalitions with other churches, social service agencies, and political groups. The name of the game in renewal ministry is God's power unleashed to transform institutions as much as it changes individuals and families.

In the conclusion, entitled "A Work in Progress," some directions for renewing our church in the future are outlined briefly. This is not an exhaustive listing, but rather a sobering yet exhilarating reminder that God's transforming Spirit is unending.

Finally, the Appendix contains The Study Guide, consisting of five sessions that your church can use as they are or can modify for your specific purposes and identified needs. In the study guide a study/reflection/action model of learning is used to organize Bible study and program planning.

The action/reflection model allows each individual to explore issues in a questioning fashion and challenges the person to make *application* of the study findings to the learner's actual personal, family, community, church, and work contexts. This method may be a different experience in learning than what some congregations usually experience in their church schools or prayer/Bible study sessions. The spiritual explosion that may occur through this method may be worth the risk of charting untried seas if we honestly are seeking to discover how God may be speaking to our congregation.

As we tell our renewal story, we are fully aware of the fact that there are other pastors and congregations who have their stories to tell. Such shared learnings will contribute to our collective search to be the church in the shadow of the skyscraper and in the midst of the joys and sorrows of urban living. It is my hope that whatever approaches your church may utilize for renewal, we all remember that congregational change is a process with God's transforming Spirit leading us every step of the way.

Introduction

At the Threshold of the Twenty-First Century: The Renewal of the Black Church

At the threshold of the twenty-first century, probably the most important question facing the pilgrim people called Afro-Americans is, Will the black church survive? This is not simply a rhetorical question; the church is the single most prominent and important institution in the black community. It is both terrifying and challenging to realize that as the church goes, so goes the community, the nation, and in large measure, the world.

Much has been written about the black church as:

- an underground "invisible" institution during slavery in North America
- a vehicle of social and educational development for free women and men during Reconstruction
- a twentieth-century urban organization (especially in the major Northern cities).

Afro-American church history helps us to recognize that there is resident in the Afro-American community a religious identity[1] (a social, theological, and biblical understanding) that tends to supercede denominational labels, ecclesiastical forms, or even geographic location. In this instance we can legitimately speak of the black church.[2] Reading these and other texts on the Afro-American

19

Christian community, one can see clear evidence of the common features that unite black people. In recent decades there has been unleashed a healthy, mature ecumenical spirit of cooperation among formerly competitive religious bodies.

I also agree with C. Eric Lincoln when he contends that there is continuity between the black church and the black community precisely because the Afro-American experience and identity is molded and shaped by the powerful influence of the institutionalized black church. Lincoln said,

> The black church, then, is in some sense a "universal church," claiming and representing all blacks out of a long tradition that looks back to the time when there was only the black church to bear witness to "who" or "what" a man was as he stood at the bar of his community. The church still accepts a broad-gauge responsibility for the black community inside and outside its formal communion. No one can die "outside the black church" if he is black.[3]

Yet the notion of the indivisible connection between the church and the community is not taken as altogether obvious in some black Christian circles these days. There has been an invasion of strange ideologies and theologies that compete for the souls of unsuspecting believers. Part of the confusion is induced by the razzle-dazzle charm of the electronic preachers and their churches. These purveyors of success religion overtly and covertly promote the Christian message as an unquestioned justification for capitalism. The Christian "elect" are made to feel that they are superior to their nonchurched sisters and brothers. "Redemption and lift," as the church-growth people call it, has created untenable barriers between many black churchgoers and the communities from which they come. This issue will become increasingly tense, I believe, as the television church leadership continues to reveal, as the Wizard of Oz, just how fragile, human, and sin-scarred they are after all.

Yet in spite of all the problems that may divide Afro-American Christians, it is still true that the black church is *the* primary institution in Afro-America; hence, it has been given a sacred stewardship trust to become all it can be as an instrument of God's transforming Spirit. Yet our understanding of the black church cannot be understood only in the more generalized, global sense. What is needed is an *internal analysis* and *appraisal* of the *local black congregation.* Since the black church only will be as effective as the composite local congregations, there is a serious need today to determine how to best utilize their divine stewardship mandate and trust.

As a pastor of a struggling black congregation, I was desperately in search of viable models for doing effective urban ministry and mission. Unfortunately, many of the printed resources that were available in the mid-1970s, often were based on "supra" notions of church renewal and growth. Often laced with more than a generous share of bravado and self-congratulation, these commentaries implied that bigger means better. Quantitative church growth was the order of the day: bigger budgets, bigger buildings, bigger memberships, not to mention bigger egos. Unless I am misrepresenting them, these church growth missives often identified "easy" steps to a renewed church. Their methods and strategies presented were sometimes helpful in identifying areas of ministry that were deficient in my congregation, but by and large these works were insensitive to the issues of black church reality.

For example, much church growth literature focused attention on the spectacular numerical growth of congregations in the Sun Belt, and conveniently if not unwittingly ignored the reality of the *urban* church—especially in the inner city. Many of the models of church growth were hardly replicable in areas like Harlem, for they often assumed population in migration, readily available inexpensive land, and low construction costs for church/educational buildings. Finally, before Paul Yong Chou, Frederick Price, and other Third World evangelicals made their way into the church-growth mainstream, most of the resources were authored by middle-class white males. Their imaging of the church was frequently colored by a class, race, and sex bias, not to mention a dependence on the false notion that with the right strategy or technique whatever is "broken" in the church can be fixed.

In spite of the magnificent success of some of the congregations lifted up by the church-growth scribes, I had a sneaky suspicion that the public display of some of the religionists of the television screen was, and I humbly hush it, an *idolatrous hype.* Where were the homeless, the helpless, the single parents, the drug addicted, the unemployed, the imprisoned, the struggling working class, or for that matter, the displaced small farmer and shopkeeper and other slices of ignored and forgotten America in all the hoopla about growing churches? The answer was clear: They are "not *our* kind of people!"[4] I investigated the church-growth literature by asking, Is there a prophetic role for the contemporary church to play in advocating for and solving some of the deep-seated social, political, and economic problems in our nation and world? The answer given was, "This is not the church's business; in fact, if the local congregation becomes too involved in rigorous social service/social action programs, it will undermine its evangelistic thrust to win souls and grow the church."[5]

Strange voices of protest within me would not keep silent. *This is not biblical; it is not true to the message of the eighth-century B.C. Old Testament prophets or the ministry and mission of Jesus of Nazareth.* Besides the tendency of some church-growth advocates to clothe key social issues in theologically simplistic and all-too-often politically conservative dress, the very urban people I ministered *with* were either discounted or ignored as a peculiar variant of the church universal, or were viewed as those pathetic and psychotic ones in need of being bulldozed from hell and damnation.

It only was after a careful reading of Ralph H. Elliott's

important work, *Church Growth That Counts,*[6] that I got in touch with a perspective that I had intuitively known. Eliott helped me to recognize, as my colleagues in Latin American-based communities understand all too well, that every congregation needs a "picture" that is a contextualized understanding of its work in the world.[7] The church might do well to recognize the fact that it deals with *real* people, in a *particular* location, with their *collective* sense of history and tradition. Eliott's challenge was that he helped to raise my consciousness regarding the special work that the church-in-the-city must perform through its particular roles as advocate (the prophetic function) and as nurturer (the priestly function). In 1976–1977 the Memorial Church was in a radically shrinking community, with a population decrease from 1970–1980 of 93,282—a twenty percent decline in area residents.* What also was true for us was that as the population in Harlem declined, so did the number of middle-income persons. They moved to suburban areas in Westchester County, Long Island, and Queens or they acquired other apartments or homes in the Southern and Northern Bronx areas. Obviously, as the constituency base moves farther from the church community, it leaves an ever-increasing number of persons with special needs and problems (i.e., substance abuse and poor health conditions, unemployment, fractured families). The local community of faith cannot with spiritual integrity ignore or deny these realities. The weak, defenseless, and oppressed individual, family, or neighborhood also is "our kind of people."

Indeed, Jesus of Nazareth challenges the church—including the black church—to take up its role as prophet-advocate for the downtrodden and abused.

> "The Spirit of the Lord is upon me,
> because he has anointed me to
> preach good news to the poor.

*In 1980 the population of Harlem was 466,418.

He has sent me to proclaim release
    to the captives
and recovering of sight to the blind,
to set at liberty those who are
    oppressed,
to proclaim the acceptable year of
    the Lord."

Luke 4:18–19

1

Tension

Memorial Baptist Church Inc., of New York City was organized on November 10, 1935, in the throes of the Great Depression. Like many churches Memorial began as a vision. It became reality in the mind of Rev. Dr. Winfred Willard Monroe, a street preacher and Scotland-trained minister. "Brother Monroe," as he called himself, was a staff associate of the historic Abyssinian Baptist Church of Harlem under the pastoral leadership of Dr. Adam Clayton Powell, Sr.[1] From a historical perspective it is clear that Rev. Monroe was well regarded by Dr. Powell Sr., but internal leadership changes in the Abyssinian Church led Rev. Monroe to organize a church of his own. The name "Memorial" was selected by a Jamaican-born member of Abyssinian, Mary Nimard, as a way of commemorating all those whom Brother Monroe had buried. He did not want a church named after him, such as "Monroe Memorial," the original name proposed by Mrs. Nimard.

Memorial began as a so-called storefront church. Its membership consisted of a handful of former Abyssinian congregants plus a few more persons from the streets of Harlem whom Rev. Monroe had led to the Lord. This fiery minister and leader was well known throughout the country for his extensive bereavement ministry. He sometimes performed an unbelievable five-to-seven funerals a day. This was due to his renowned eulogies, poetic sensitivity, and (some would say) his ability to gain entrance for the deceased into heaven. Rev. Monroe would quip, "I do not get anyone into heaven. I only take them to the gate. Then it's between them and Saint Peter!"

Rev. Monroe also grew in reputation because he frequented taverns and restaurants in order to gain support for his now-growing church. Barmaids, "numbers policy" bankers, and a host of those untouched by the Protestant church of the 1930s and early 1940s regarded Rev. Monroe as "their" pastor and gave invaluable financial support to his movement and ministry. After about six years the Memorial congregation had to be housed in its larger, present quarters at 141 West 115th Street, Central Harlem, New York. In the 1950s the Memorial Church peaked at a membership of over 600 persons under Rev. Monroe's leadership. It could boast of a thriving Sunday school, three choirs, a large youth department, a board of deacons of some twenty persons, a radio ministry that was heard throughout the length and breadth of the city, a nationally known anthem choir with paid soloists, a vibrant missionary society, and innumerable clubs and auxiliaries. For thirty-six years Rev. Monroe kept the Memorial ship afloat with the help of almighty God.

Then a stroke incapacitated the organizer of the flock. Little by little, the membership began to decrease due to death, retirement back to the South, and disinterest now that the eloquent spokesperson of God was ailing and near death. After thirty-six years as the spiritual leader, Rev. Monroe slipped away to "the land of perfect day." The church continued, but its membership dropped to less than 150 persons. During the three-year search for a pastor, the diaconate continued to provide leadership in the church. Under the direction of its chairperson, the church remained unified and continued to worship. But the decay was radical. Little was left of Dr. Monroe's dream except a badly maintained building and a handful of the remnant congregation of mostly retired senior adults.

Long pastorates, such as Dr. Monroe's, create incredible difficulties for the succeeding pastor. Yet, to his everlasting credit, Rev. George P. Polk, a trained pastoral counseling supervisor, skillfully and creatively ministered to a dying congregation and results began to show. The church was painted, new hymnbooks and Bibles were purchased, and a scholarship fund for young people was organized (suggesting that a few teenagers now were joining the church again). A Bible class was established in which persons studied the theology of some of the fathers and mothers of the church of yesterday and today.

It was during the three-year pastorate of Dr. Polk that I frequently was invited to preach on Sunday mornings. Actually, George Polk and I became ministerial partners at Harlem Interfaith Counseling Services, where I served as a pastoral counselor-in-training. Memorial members saw me in the pulpit enough times to come to realize my style of delivery, commitment to the church, and feelings about some of the issues affecting Harlem and the world community. During his third pastoral year, Rev. Polk was called to a new pastoral counseling position in Washington, D.C. I was selected to immediately assume the pastorate of Memorial in August 1976.

The first pastoral year was trying, indeed. Though I was voted in as pastor by all but two votes, many members thought I was too young (twenty-six), and too inexperienced to pastor a "major" Baptist church in Harlem. Although this *was* my first pastorate, I had been preaching and serving the church since the age of thirteen.

I was licensed into the ministry when I was sixteen years old. I was blessed with the training of my East Harlem childhood pastor, Rev. Jacob Hillery; and in later years by Dr. Gardner C. Taylor, minister of Concord Baptist Church of Christ, Brooklyn; and Dr. Earl B. Moore, minister of St. Paul's Baptist Church, Harlem. To these men and the innumerable saints of the black Christian church, I owe much in my preparation for the ministry. They allowed me the opportunity to visit the sick and organize youth programs, summer vacation Bible schools, counseling ministries for young adults, and leader training conferences and retreats. They also all gave me countless opportunities to lead in worship and deliver sermons.

Union Theological Seminary in New York City was the place where my theology was tested, my biblical foundations analyzed, and my sense of vocation and calling weighed.

Sitting through an ordination council organized by the United Missionary Baptist Association (National Baptist U.S.A., Inc.) exposed me to the need to overcome my tendency to use terms that needed constant clarification for the people in the pew. The pastors and ministers who led me through the ordeal of ordination made me conscious of the need to make the gospel "plain" and understandable to those who may have never attended seminary but who theologize every day of their working lives. They helped me understand, at least in part, what they call "Negro-ology": the ability to relate to the particular and peculiar needs of Afro-American Christians.

Pastor New—What Do You Do?

I was Pastor New. The members already had blessed my ministry with a fine installation service that lasted four hours. There were more than sixty pastors and ministers present, not including the 600 personal friends and church and family members who also were in attendance.

But trouble was brewing at the installation service. During my remarks I confessed that I saw my task as enabling necessary changes both within the church and in the community. It was stated that the church could not remain isolated from its community or the world. At a church service filled by so many ecclesiastical giants, it would be difficult and inappropriate to publicly ask the new spiritual leader for clarification of his remarks. There is always a "later," and it came quickly. It was a tension-filled "later."

Church people are an interesting group. In my years of experience in the local parish, it has been rare for people to come forward and pointedly say: "Reverend, you were chosen because we thought you would help us to keep our church just the way it's always been!" They rather say things like, "Reverend, so-and-so *never* did this," or "I remember when we *used* to do this or that."

The struggle of my early years in pastoring was not the result of one or two difficult members. It was centered around a conflict of vision. For some of the older members, it was not that they could not see. It was rather that theirs was a *backward gaze;* mine was, more or less, a *forward look.* In other words, many members cherished their rich history, accomplishments, and reputation. But they luxuriated in that history without seeming interested or concerned about possibilities for their church in the present and the future. I had not traveled the long trek of this congregation from Depression days. My interest was to move the congregation forward—to challenge it to engage in outreach ministries in the community. I was trying to move too soon. I was anxious to get the church to first base, but they had not yet left the locker room. What really was happening was that they were still in a pastoral bereavement stage, having lost Dr. Monroe to death and Rev. Polk to another job. Unfortunately, I was not the slightest bit aware of this and was deeply hurt every time I heard from some innocent soul how personable and committed a leader Dr. Monroe was. Just when I thought that some of the "Monroe-ites" were ready to accept me as their pastor, a person would publicly pray, asking the Lord to bless "their pastor," quickly adding; "I mean Rev. Monroe," even though he was dead!

There always is the tendency of the new pastor to fight the ghosts of the former ministers—especially that one individual like Winfred Willard Monroe, who looms larger than life in the consciousness of the membership. This posture proved disastrous. Had I recognized that many persons in the church were yet grieving the death of a significant former leader; had I known that they were looking back because the memories in their minds lived on as if they had happened only yesterday; had I known that there are integrity, beauty, and accomplishments that are part of yesteryear; I might have been less forceful in imposing my vision of tomorrow so quickly.

After all, Jesus teaches us to respect those who grieve— even their deceased ministers: "Blessed are those who mourn . . ." (Matthew 5:4). Yet I was driven by the need for change in our church based on objective facts, not the least of which was a physically and spiritually dying congregation and a community where former thriving buildings now were boarded up and stripped of people, pipes, and boilers. But objective facts alone cannot win people if they are not yet ready to move in response to change the negative realities.

Like the Memorial of my early pastorate, many congregations are dying. Just as fruit withers on the vine, the death is often not sudden or even apparent.

Some juice of life might still be left, hidden in the deepest recesses of the congregational soul. However, the telltale signs of decay slowly begin to show:

1. *Major fluctuations and/or reductions in church attendance:* Membership loyalty is minimal. They involve themselves in the life of the congregation only in limited ways. For example, the Sunday morning worship attendance is unpredictable. This may be due to a number of factors, such as the historical tendency of the congregation to attend worship only on "important" Sundays, as when the Lord's Supper is served or a revival is rendered. Otherwise, one may either attend another church or stay home.

2. *More deaths of old congregants than membership of new ones:* Often, membership deaths occur in cycles: a few at a

time, and then a refreshing period when no one dies. But in a radically deteriorated situation, especially when the major portion of the membership is elderly, funerals may be celebrated more than baby dedications, marriages, or receptions of new members.

3. *Struggles to meet the basic cash-flow needs:* One sign of this is the "emergency offering" syndrome that exists when members do not give sufficient monetary gifts to keep the church going. It is represented by a special envelope, an added potluck supper, and often all too much attention given to this roller-coaster financial condition from the pulpit. There is created an atmosphere of weekly desperation and anger toward those who refuse to increase their giving.

4. *Boredom in worship:* It's the same noncreative ritual each week. This is especially deadly where there are no allowances given for genuine participation by the congregation. "It's what's up front that counts," that is, the worship service is dominated by the pulpit and the choir and often generates a lack of sincere interest in what's going on among the pew members.

5. *Demoralized, "burned-out" leadership:* "Leaders for life" is one major manifestation of this problem. Their theme song is "I shall not be moved!" even though they often are given to public complaint about "all" they have to do at the church or how *no one* can be found to take their place. Or, leaders in the church, even in a rotational system, are not affirmed, praised, or supported; or conversely, they are constantly condemned, upbraided, or chastised in sermons, at business meetings, and so forth because of their insufficiencies.

6. *Congregational struggles, often reflected in trivial interpersonal conflicts:* Congregations all too infrequently allow a member to air his or her grievances or disagreements with another member. The bitterness then festers

until there is a contagious negativity that is carried in the souls of these people, sometimes for many years. The dilemma is that this animosity often affects church programming, especially when those who are angry or hurt are in the forefront of leadership or are the unofficial "movers-and-shakers" in the congregation.

7. *A "them versus us" sense of the world—viewing the community and the larger world context as essentially unredeemable.* The religious creed perpetrated is that the Christian believer is representative of a "saved remnant." Through proclamation and teaching a "holier-than-thou" attitude, members see themselves and their congregation as the only *true* people of God. Other denominations, and especially the unsaved people in the community, are doomed to hell and damnation. In this context the church "walls" itself in, services only its members, and provides no opportunities for coalition building with other non-Christian groups, or fellowship with churches of other denominations.

8. *A lack of innovation in worship.* In this instance worship is predictable and routine. One can stay home on Sundays and pretty much determine what is happening at the church at any given time. Besides the routine nature of the service, there are no creative approaches tried to invigorate the membership and allow worship to be a celebrative and/or deliberate experience. People "go through the motions" but they are not challenged or changed in the process.

9. *Survival ploys to save the building at the expense of ministry and mission.* The entire church leadership effort is to support building expenses. There is no intentional budgetary commitment to ministry and mission beyond the church's four walls, or there are only token gifts given through denominational and/or parachurch groups to emergency mission causes (for example, Ethiopian famine relief).

Not any one of these above signs alone is indicative of a dying church, but usually a combination of five or six telltale evidences suggests the last breath of an organization experiencing a "sickness unto death." In my first pastoral year, Memorial was experiencing all nine of the above signs of decay. It was on the critical list and in need of immediate intensive care.

Here was our challenge: How do the pastor and leaders of a church honestly confront the imminent death of their congregation and move quickly enough to seek its renewal and growth? How might a church develop in spite of, or better yet, *change with,* those faithful, committed persons who righteously cling to their "holy" past?

For a long time these questions could not be even remotely answered, let alone discussed. Again, our congregation was yet mourning the death of Rev. Monroe. Initiatives related to the new pastor's salary and benefits package or even the creation of a parsonage (the church never owned a manse) were met with, "Rev. Monroe *never* depended on us to support him! He knew we were poor people on fixed incomes, so he got his friends in the streets to support him *and* this church." I had nothing against the streets, per se, but for the life of me I could not understand how a group of church people could expect their minister to depend on those outside the church to be his bread-and-butter supporters, especially if he cast his lot with a church needing to reverse its adverse circumstances.

Unsnarling the Pastor's "Package" Dilemma

The straw that nearly broke the camel's back was related to the agreement by the pulpit committee and the boards to pay me a specific annual salary. The initial agreement was rescinded and reduced by several thousand dollars. The explanation was the church did not have *that* kind of money. Six months later, the original amount was reinstated. The explanation was the church now is doing a little better financially, so we can afford to pay you what you asked for. I recently had graduated from seminary, so this financial roller-coaster thrust my family into incredible economic difficulty. Memorial was struggling for its survival—and so was my household. The crisis made both my church and my home uncomfortable environments. Sometimes I was tempted to avoid going to either of them.

This was just one of innumerable friction periods in the early years. The parsonage, the benefits, and the salary eventually came through, but only after long, bitter, and often humiliating public conflicts between the pastor and some of the leaders, or even between the pastor and some unexpected members.

Somehow, I could not help but believe that deep down many of our church people also were hurt by the early conflicts. Their glances, their private words of support, and their donations of desserts, household utensils, and money were the tangible evidences that there were many among them who cared deeply about me and my family.

Part of the reason why this issue was not properly handled was because our church was an "independent" Baptist church. It did not have access to the important expertise of a denominational staff like ABC. It was a year after I began my pastorate in 1977 that our church decided to become dually aligned with the American Baptist Churches, U.S.A., and the National Baptist Convention, U.S.A., Inc.

It is important for new pastors to make certain that their financial arrangements are clearly worked out in advance of assuming the pastoral ministry. An important ingredient in the preparation of the ministerial salary/package is the involvement of the denominational office. The area minister or staff executive of a regional office can share with pulpit committees and congregations their broader understanding of what other churches are contributing to maintain the pastoral leadership. Especially in cases where the new pastor must find her or his own home or apartment, the denominational office can do much to sensitize the congregation to present market rentals or home purchasing prices.

It should be noted that pastors who have been in their same charge for a number of years often are in need of periodic salary/package review. When a leader must sing for his or her own supper, it can give people the impression that one is an opportunist or simply overly concerned about money. The recent creation of pastoral relations committees in some churches may be a helpful way for congregations to take responsibility for determining their pastors' personal and family financial needs each year.

To Flee or Not to Flee?

It's a fact that hurt often blinds us; we can neither recognize nor affirm our support base. So it remains inert and silent as we plunge more deeply into the midnight-hour tear ritual. I knew I was "called" of God to minister to urban persons. I was convinced, initially, that Memorial was the setting for the realization of a viable mission of love and nurturing in Harlem and the city. The problem was I could not get to the heart of the matter: the needed renewal of this potentially great congregation. My personal needs and the survival needs of the congregation seemed antithetical, mutually exclusive.

After a year of pastoring, I was prepared to leave my work at the church and find employment in a more lucrative field of endeavor.

This tension-laden period kept me on my knees, though, and faithful in the regular reading of Scripture. During one tear-drenched night, I opened my Bible, and like a lightning-flash, the words of Isaiah 40:30–31 (KJV) broke into my consciousness with new power and clarity:

> Even the youths shall faint and be weary, and the young men shall utterly fall: but they that wait upon the LORD shall renew *their* strength; They shall mount up with wings as eagles; They shall run, and not be weary; *and* they shall walk, and not faint."

In the Hebrew sense, "waiting" is an active anticipation of the coming of the Holy Spirit. God's Spirit ministers to us. It imparts to the believer strength we did not even know was there. Waiting is an acceptance of our incapacity to "pull off" real, lasting change by our limited strength alone. We need more—a compelling, divine "more."

Waiting also does something else. Those of us prone to rush things to get desired results or run away are forced to slow down long enough to really hear and experience *our* people. We come to sense *their* aspirations, *their* strengths, *their* faith patterns, *their* needs. We come to know them as far more resourceful than we initially realized. Such is the power of God's transforming Spirit. Such was the discovery at my tension-laden church in Central Harlem. That upsetting Holy Spirit broke through in my own life and forced me to reevaluate my decision to throw in the towel.

There is a paradox in Christian service. Sometimes we cannot be most useful to God's kingdom purposes when all the doors of opportunity are opened to us at once. Often, a slammed or even a locked door may be a necessary obstacle in our lives in order for us to learn new truths about ourselves and about those who are part of our ministry. I, a seminary-trained pastor, did not have a full understanding of how to unlock the shut door of my congregation. Since I could not run away from this challenge, I prayed and prayed some more, waiting for a clue from God.

In prayerful, anticipatory waiting, an inner voice slowly began to demand a hearing. It said to me in no uncertain terms that I had not really recognized the humanity of each member; that each person was a unique gift from God. Therefore, my image of the church had to be smashed, for I wrongly saw it as an *organization* with me at the head as corporation president. The Spirit revealed that I needed a fresh look at God's church as a living, vibrant, interconnected, and interdependent *organism* with Jesus at the helm. People, the Spirit noted, often do not respond to challenges if they do not feel that they are being listened to, cared for, or loved. The relentless inner voice continued: *My commitment to move the church forward was commendable, but with what purpose or mission in mind? Was I not unconsciously in awe of the phenomenal success of other churches in our neighborhood and nation, uncritically trying to duplicate their programs without a careful recognition of our congregation's uniqueness and distinctives?* The Spirit of God not only began to transform the church, but also the pastor as well. What was at stake for me was an awakened recognition that a new minister should first cultivate the *priestly* and *pastoral* dimension of one's vocation before charging *ahead of* the troops in *prophetic* confrontations. At least that was *my* challenge in ministry at Memorial.

With David, I could proclaim: "I waited patiently on the Lord, and God heard my cry!" (Psalm 40:1, paraphrased). Prayer invigorated my soul. My attitude became less anxious and fearful. My sense of God's call was sharpened. The prayerful waiting on God lifted me from the spiritual valley of despair and transported me by divine energy to new heights of commitment to our dying parish. Not that the pain and hurt had magically disappeared. What was critical was that now I knew that I had a purpose and a calling to work in partnership with the people of Memorial. When there is a partnership between the pulpit and the pew in ministry, the congregational storms begin to subside.

Resisting the Temptation to Flee: Personal Pastoral Prayer

It was through prayer that I discovered the importance of "planting seeds and trusting the promise" of God. Through prayer I became more disciplined, more deliberate, and more patient with the pastoral work I was called upon to render. Through prayer the Spirit nudges the preacher to capture the vision of God, not just to improve her or his particular local church or to deepen one's spiritual life, but to enhance, enrich, and expand the kingdom of God.

While seeking to renew Memorial Church, prayer led me to see the far-larger context of the goals of the kingdom of

God. Even if some program failed to come to pass, the sense of the overall strategy of God's work was what was needed in order to resist the temptation to flee.

Prayer planning is a central ingredient in keeping the pulpit and pew sane and strong enough to continue the risky unfolding work of ministry and mission. This may sound contradictory, but the prayer discipline helped relax my ego enough so that my identity and witness would rely more on God and less on myself. It also helped me to see more good in the people to whom I was called "to minister with" than I initially had realized.

Personal pastoral prayer must become a disciplined, protected, and protracted exercise. Not only are the responsibilities of ministry ever impinging on one's time, but also the stress and strain of doing God's will in an urban environment is taxing on one's mind, body, and soul. There always is more to do in ministry, and hence, blocking out a time segment for prayer each day is a critical component of pastoral development. Here are a few suggestions for developing a pastoral prayer discipline.

1. *Manage your time.* Get a handle on your weekly schedule to determine how you might best focus your energies. For example, some pastors select one day a week for sick visitation, except in cases of emergency. Intentionally block out *an hour* each day exclusively for prayer. Put it on your calendar or in your date book.

2. *Practice prayer waiting.* One way that I have found helpful to me is to quiet myself, sit in a relaxed position, and let ideas and images race through my mind. After a point, the images began to cluster themselves together and organize into something of a unified, coherent picture. Often, one begins to see people in the congregation in new ways—in connection to a troubled family member or in need of special attention, for example. Or one begins to pinpoint more effective

ways to reach out to a person who does not say much but has gifts to share with the congregation.

3. *Experience prayer lament.* There are times when the pressures and problems of pastoring are so enormous that one must actively lament. From 1985 to 1986 I conducted forty-five funerals of black males who died from or were killed in drug-related cases. After a point I could not hold it any longer. Like the Hebrews of old, I developed my own "wailing wall," a place in my home where I could shed tears and challenge God and myself to do something about this international tragedy. Every pastor as well as every believer needs a wailing wall.

4. *Create a prayer partnership.* Networking is the name of the game these days. Even pastors need others to share in intercessory prayer. One pastor I know meets each week with a small group of members at the church at 6 A.M. for prayer. This group changes and so do the concerns that surface. Often the pastor is exclusively prayed for by this small group. Other pastors select colleagues in ministry or friends not connected to their church community to share in prayer. One's spouse or children also should be considered as prayer partners.

5. *Do Bible study.* The scramble to get a sermon or Sunday school lesson prepared each week often deflects from Bible study. I mention Bible study in the context of prayer because many times a quiet, nonutilitarian reading of Scripture helps us to vicariously identify with the struggles and triumphs of men and women of faith, which in turn gives us handles for doing ministry where we are.

6. *Practice directed prayer.* How do we solve a problem or handle a particular issue in the congregation, in the community, or in one's personal life? Name the issue clearly, lift it up verbally to God, and make petition. Sometimes we do not get answers to concerns because

we are not specific in our requests. Be specific. God will respond, and sometimes even a no answer may prove to be a blessing. Prayer helped me to back my engine so that I could hook up with the people of Memorial in a joint venture in ministry. This meant coming to know and understand them, and they me, before seeking to enact policies, programs, and processes for church renewal.

Readers who are not pastors or ministers also might try some of the prayer disciplines noted or share these ideas with their spiritual leaders. The pastor might be relieved to know that a congregant is willing to share in one's unfolding ministry.

2

Prayer Power!

Prayer is the key to church renewal. As we already noted, those engaged in pastoral ministry certainly must cultivate a disciplined prayer life. But so must those in the pew. Too many church prayer meetings are helter-skelter events without intentionality or design. The goal of prayer is empowerment—to "call down" the kingdom of God into the lives of lay members and ministers and into the congregation's collective life. Communal prayer helps us to overcome our self-centeredness and begin to focus attention on the needs of the other persons in the group, their family concerns, and issues that affect the neighborhood or the community at large. In our prayer clusters we have those among us who are sick, have special needs, or have experienced a celebrative moment (a wedding anniversary, birthday, graduation, baptism, and so forth). It is important to focus attention on special issues lifted up in the group, such as the selection of a new black chancellor to run the New York City school system, or teenagers killed in Nicaragua and South Africa. We also focus on issues within our congregation.

Organizing for Prayer Time in the Local Church

It seems to be during the periods of tremendous travail for the church and the persecution of its prophetic leadership that prayer becomes an important renewal and empowering reality for God's people. Prayer is always a critical necessity for the community of faith. The specific tensions and troubles induced by change in a renewing congregation make prayer an even more urgent necessity for both the *change agents* and the *change resisters.*

Organizing and/or reshaping prayer time in a local church ought to be rendered with the utmost care. Most congregations that I have analyzed, including my own, have experienced a renewal of commitment and involvement in kingdom-building when the prayer discipline is emphasized from the pulpit, intentionally included in the weekly schedule of the church, and made a *priority* in church programming.

It is wise for congregations to seek the maximum involvement of the membership in the prayer meetings. How might this be accomplished?

1. *Leadership:* Different clubs, auxiliaries, boards, or selected individuals might be chosen to lead in the devotionals, select the music, and design the general format for the prayer time. There is more effectiveness in having an overall coordinator and co-coordinator of the prayer event.

2. *Publicity:* Proper publicity of the prayer time is vital. Getting the congregation on board and enthusiastic about organized, disciplined prayer time must have the public support of the pulpit, the officers, and the key leaders of the congregation. Bulletin announcements, colorful fliers, signs, and commitment letters also work wonders.

3. *Programming:* Flexibility is an essential ingredient in maximizing the effectiveness of the prayer time. There is no reason under heaven why the prayer meeting *must* be on a Wednesday or Friday night just because these time frames may have been appropriate in other settings or in another age. Part of the reason

why prayer time has not been as effective in many urban areas as in the South is because the work habits of church members have shifted like the rest of the population. Many people do not work Monday to Friday from 9 A.M. to 5 P.M. Prayer opportunities in small *koinonia* or *prayer cluster groups* might best be scheduled at convenient times for working members. Hospital staff, for example, may require an early morning prayer service rather than an evening experience. Prayer clusters may best be made available according to the lifestyles and work habits of city dwellers.

In our setting, we concluded that four prayer meetings were required, given the life pulse of our congregation. First, there is a midweek, noon prayer service/Bible study for mostly retired senior citizens and those who work at night. This group is facilitated by a diaconate member and a minister. The diaconate chairperson and another lay leader conduct a second Bible study/prayer session one evening each week. Still another diaconate member and lay leader provide a third weekly prayer service in the evening in a nearby housing project one block from our church. The tenants in that public housing development *would not walk one block* in our neighborhood to attend Bible study and prayer services, but do regularly attend sessions in a church member's apartment in their own building. Here refreshments are shared and much individual counseling, affirmation, and support take place. The fourth meeting follows Sunday morning services, when teenagers age thirteen to seventeen meet in their own prayer/Bible study circle coordinated by our minister of youth.

4. *Creativity:* As already suggested, our church developed a prayer service/Bible study format to gain greater participation and to provide for the spiritual formation of the membership. During the warm months we

also conduct intercessory prayer services on the street corner next to our church. There were some young men selling drugs on our street. A small group of prayer service attendees suggested that we go to the corner, create a circle, and pray one at a time. The drug sellers were so overwhelmed by our public display of love for them—we invited them to join us in prayer—that they moved their business to another location! Also in the creativity process, time is allotted for spontaneous songs, brief prayers, testimonies (sharing of life stories), or other creative expressions such as reading poetry or learning a new song. Then we enter into the Bible study portion of the session. We might select a book to study in depth, isolate a life theme and find applications in the biblical record, or select specific passages for review. After the participants have successfully completed the biblical training for that segment, they receive a certificate that is presented on a Sunday morning.

5. *Explication:* Many church members will not attend prayer services. This often is because most congregations traditionally have a few leaders and members whose public prayers are vital and vibrant. The majority of the congregation may opt *not* to attend the prayer experience for fear that they will be called upon to pray and be unable to match the profound oratory of their more verbal brothers and sisters.[1]

Opportunities must be sought to give the shy, inarticulate, or embarrassed individual[2] a chance to both learn how to pray and feel a sense of permission from the prayer cluster group to express one's self in a way that is most comfortable to that person. Silent prayer time or prepared prayers also may prove helpful to those left out of the prayer life of the church. Pastors and lay leaders who are sensitive to those left out of the prayer life of the church also might quietly and discreetly offer these individuals private coaching or select for them more experienced spiritual brothers/sisters or prayer partners to help fortify their prayer life.

6. *Pastoral coordination and participation:* It did not take long for me to realize that if we were to have flexible prayer services that worked in our church context, I could not be present at all of them, let alone conduct them. My present role regarding the prayer clusters is to stay tuned to their progress; provide their diaconate lay and ministerial leadership with support and public encouragement during worship and meeting times; and provide ongoing training in Bible study and prayer coordination through the churchwide vision group, which I presently conduct on two Saturdays each month. I will say more about the development of the pastor's vision group later. From time to time I attend one of the prayer services, but I try my best to keep as quiet as possible to allow the general dynamics operative in these settings to continue without interference. This method also has given persons "safe space" to grow as leaders and to increasingly become partners with the pastor in lay nurture and support. In addition, the prayer time, if skillfully conducted, can open up avenues for more trusting relationships. For example, people in prayer often discover that they have similar problems or concerns, and may exchange telephone numbers to share stories and develop informal support systems.

7. *Evaluation:* One major problem of the decentralized core prayer services/Bible study concept is that midweek worship service for a large portion of the membership often does not take place. The groups are small in size, ranging from ten to thirty people in attendance at a given time. Also, the leader/pastor is forced to give up the notion that she or he can be present at every prayer service given the fact that time flexibility is for the convenience of the constituents.

Though three of the four prayer/Bible study sessions are held in our church building, perhaps the day will come when many more prayer sessions will be conducted in peoples' homes or community centers, especially for those who live a distance from our church. Perhaps these decentralized prayer and Bible study clusters will become increasingly difficult. Then the notion of the Memorial building as the focus of the congregation's life increasingly will be stretched. However, all things considered, I would rather the excitement of prayer/Bible cluster growth away from the church building than to put new wine into old prayer-time wineskins and witness a waning of lay enthusiasm and commitment to grow in grace and power.

Operation Prayer Power!
Training the Facilitators

Intentional scheduling of prayer time in the church can offer exciting possibilities for renewal and growth of the pastor and the membership. But there needs to be ongoing training of the prayer leaders to help them develop their gifts and talents in creatively facilitating these important events. Here are some suggestions for selecting and training prayer facilitators:

1. *Select leaders who are committed to prayer.* It makes sense to select persons who are themselves convinced about the power of prayer to lead prayer clusters. These persons should be consistent in their commitment and be able to attract others to join them in prayer time. At Memorial lay and ministerial leaders, both male and female, are selected to facilitate the prayer groups. We also are sensitive to the need to have several groups not only for time convenience, but also because of age differences. (For example, there is a teen group who pray and study Scripture together.) An important point to remember is that the leader of

the prayer group really is a facilitator. She or he calls the group together, structures the use of time, and allows the participants to fully share in the process. The participants must be helped to feel a sense of ownership of the prayer group.

2. *Train prayer facilitators.* The prayer facilitator may need to become familiar with basic lay shepherding skills.[3] The facilitator must be assisted to come to identify the needs, struggles, and strengths of those engaged in prayer. As a lay shepherd the facilitator can help the new members learn how to pray and assist youth and children in developing prayer discipline.

Part of the facilitator's training is to develop a job description so that they can better understand their ministerial task. A facilitator:

- nurtures an atmosphere where all participants feel that they "own" a part of the group process.
- assists each person to feel that his or her ideas are valued, even if they must be lovingly corrected.
- is not a star but is rather like a "coach" who leads to get a response from "the team" (Bible study group).
- seeks to gain the support of inactive, bored, disgruntled, or neglected participants.
- reflects an awareness of *group dynamics.* Some group dynamics are resistance, anger, boredom, distrust, and jealousy among participants. Check out *body language.*
- helps the group to work through the problem by identifying it, asking the group members to state their individual feelings about what is taking place (including nonverbalized concerns), and then seeking a solution.
- is willing to be nonjudgmental. You are not called to force people to accept your truth (no matter how right you may be). Through trust and acceptance you will lead them to grow into truthful living. The fact that

they are with you in the same room is proof that they are there to learn, grow, and mature in faith. Among all age groups, adults are the least likely to consciously waste their time.

- is willing to be vulnerable and never appears to others as self-righteous, for this is un-Christian. Besides, if you know everything, how did you manage to remain on earth? Being vulnerable means being open to criticism; open enough to be challenged without caving in; open enough to be evaluated by the group, even if their analysis forces us to change our teaching techniques and methods of sharing.*

3. *Affirm prayer facilitators.* The prayer facilitators regularly should be celebrated in the church, from the pulpit, in the bulletin or newsletter. They are important partners in ministry for they are often the first ones to become aware of problems, crises, and joys among the membership.

Black Christians often state that "prayer changes things." Prayer frequently changes the conditions and circumstances of our lives. But prayer also changes *people*—most especially the kingdom-bearers, the change agents of God. It was through dialogue with God that this product of the 1960s, this activist preacher, became still long enough to recognize a profound revelation: He was *not* God, nor was he a failure in the ministry. I heard Jesus say to me in the fresh, clear call of openness to God's Spirit, "Let *My will* be done on earth as it is in heaven!" This is no mere rhetorical device. Prayer taps the power source of the Spirit and invigorates pulpit *and* pew to become engaged in the risky business of church renewal.

*Note: This description can apply to persons who undertake various forms of ministry such as young adult ministries, Bible study, and so forth. The term "facilitator" is not always a recognizable title in some churches. Though we used this term for two or more years, we presently use the term "coordinator" because our constituents relate better to this title. The title has changed but the task remains the same.

The ultimate "pull" of prayer led some of us at Memorial to come to hear and trust one another. Prayer also served to empower some individuals who never before spoke in public, or who never felt comfortable in exercising leadership in the church, to become more involved in the life and ministry of the church.

3

Transformation

Prayer was the starting point in leading Memorial out of its spiritual morass. In the midst of all the resistance I encountered as Pastor New, I became sensitized to the fact that there were many congregants—the "church pillars"—and many of the newer members who joined after I assumed the pastorate, who really *did* want their church to be revitalized. A good part of the reason why they were beginning to earnestly desire renewal was because they had, through prayer, an opportunity to grow closer to one another. A preliminary sense of trust had taken hold of our church. As people are ministered to in prayer, their personal burdens are lifted and they are empowered to tackle issues beyond their private concerns. What's more, though I do not now attend all the varied prayer clusters, in the beginning of my pastorate I made it a point to teach a Bible lesson and share my ministry and life concerns at at least one prayer meeting each week. People began to grow closer to me as they recognized that like them, I also was in need of intercessory prayer. Through the changing of our attitudes, transformation slowly began to happen. Once we relaxed our defenses we were able to actively discern God's will for our church. We now were ripe for new ministry possibilities in Harlem. In fact, we now were in search of a vision that celebrated the healthy accomplishments of the past while launching us into heretofore uncharted arenas of ministry and mission.

Can We Talk?

The people of our church, that blessed remnant, simply needed to know that their rich history was not being steam-rolled by forced change. There was need to affirm the accomplishments of the past while also seeking common areas of agreement between the pastor and the people.

A famous comedienne often asks the question, "Can we talk?" Prayer sets the stage for not only an openness to God's transforming Spirit, but it also slowly sensitizes us to the need to open ourselves to greater communication with one another.

As the burdens of my first pastoral year began to lift, many new people began to fellowship with our church (over 100 in the first two years). This created innumerable tensions, but a healthy concern emerged. Many of the older members and leaders suggested that we organize a group. Actually, the group at first was a cluster of concerned members—older and newer ones—who wanted to talk about the conditions of our church. Months later, after we were well into the process of communicating, someone suggested that what we really were doing was "searching for a vision." The group seemed to resonate when the word "vision" was used, so after much debate, the name selected for the cluster was the "Vision Group." What's important to realize is that the name for the group grew out of our experiences together in dialogue.

The Composition of the Group

The Vision Group was larger than most clusters of its type; some twenty-to-thirty people attended each bi-monthly meeting. Most renewal manuals tend to recommend between eight and twelve people for such a process. We left membership to this group open to anyone who wished to become a part of it. This was done so that no one would feel that they had been excluded or intentionally overlooked. The Vision Group was a remarkable cluster of new members as well as seasoned churchgoers. The diaconate, trustee board, missionaries, service organization leadership, and a few unaffiliated members were well represented. Young adults and senior citizens were equally involved. Two teenagers were consistent attendees.

The group met for approximately one-and-a-half years. Its purpose was to discover necessary changes that had to take place in our congregation in order for us to grow. After the Vision Group ended, it took several years to put in motion some of our intentional program goals.

Preparation

The Vision Group proved to be an immediate success in our church because it took place twice monthly on Saturdays and was limited to two-and-a-half hours each session. Saturdays proved the best possible time for maximum participation at our church because we were able to piggyback the Vision Group with other club, auxiliary, and group meetings and choir rehearsal.

The Vision Group was announced each week in the church bulletin and from the pulpit and placed on the monthly agendas of the diaconate, trustees, and the leaders' council (a group of auxiliary, service, and club presidents) to solicit their participation.

The Vision Group grew by word of mouth as participants began to express enthusiasm for the special experiences of sharing and learning they encountered. A church might find it helpful to write each member a letter to encourage participation or construct a prominent sign or display to announce the group's formation. Still another approach is to assign a member each week to recruit participants. Also, some churches have found that a more viable option for their needs is to select one person from each board of the church and laypersons representing a wide cross-section of the church (being sensitive to age, sex, and vocational diversity).

Though coordinated by me, the Vision Group was an open forum with increasing involvement and participation from the members. The typical two-and-a-half-hour segment would be fashioned as follows.

For the sake of this resource book, I will detail some of the learnings from the discussion and fellowship, Bible study, and church growth strategies segments. Focusing on our evolving training/sharing events in the Vision Group might be helpful to you in developing a format for your congregation's preparation.

Discussion and Fellowship

Initially, I was the instructor of the Vision Group. After a few months leaders with a variety of gifts emerged from the group. They often shared with me in team teaching. I taught classes on the function of the church, the call of people into a variety of ministries, leadership, and stewardship development. For many months the basic Bible study proved to be less important than the orientation and fellowship times. It was clear that most people, even those who had been in the church most of their lives, only knew one another in rather limited ways. They were hungry to discover new information about those persons with whom they occupied seats in the same pews! Often, I wanted to rush past these times of fellowship in order to get to the content of Bible facts and church growth concepts, but thank heaven, the group was resistant and would linger for long periods telling their personal stories of tragedy and triumph. These were magnificent moments of sharing for all of us.

These were most productive sessions, for they not only allowed new and old members to become acquainted with one another, but I also became closer to the leaders and new members in ways that would have otherwise taken many more years to materialize.

Whenever groups allow individuals to speak *their* truth, there is a noticeable increase in tolerance toward those who are not a part of the congregational mainstream, i.e., the church leadership. Listening skills increase as well, for in group process only one person at a time can speak. They unwittingly take center stage, even if this is not their "usual" role in worship or in other arenas of church life.

Church growth can occur when a *core group* or Vision Group reaches that point where they can come to know fellow church members, trust them, and share in common envisioning for the church in the world. Without this basic foundation the process of church renewal and development appears to be more an imposition or a foreign program than it is a collectively shared commitment of the body of believers to *risk* change and growth. In short, church renewal becomes an owned reality when congregational members feel a sense of common fellowship and commitment to a collective future.

Bible Study

As noted earlier, fellowship and discussion were critical concerns in the life of the Vision Group. But Bible study was an enlivening experience as well. Since the group was initiated by a cadre of members, every possible aid in fostering church renewal was seriously investigated by these "turned-on" people. When the Bible becomes a relevant, living source book and guide for Christians, church renewal and growth are inevitable by-products. When people honestly come to experience the brutal and blessed saga of Yahweh's loving, judging, liberating, and saving movement among the children of Israel; indeed, when they come face-to-face with Jesus the Christ in his healing, teaching, miracles, and preaching, something begins to happen.

It is important for the facilitator (or coordinator) to be sensitive to needs of adult learners. Is the room you are using well lighted? Are the chairs comfortable? Is your equipment, such as chalkboards, available for use? Some other rules-of-thumb in heading your group in Bible study follow.

Time Frame	The Event
12:00–12:15	The devotional period: praise power, sharing of songs, favorite devotional Bible verses, prayers, and concerns.
12:15–12:30	Discussion and fellowship. This part often was difficult to move, for once people got to know one another, the sharing of concerns would take longer than the allotted time.
12:30–1:00	Bible study.
1:00–1:15	Coffee break/informal sharing.
1:15–1:40	Church growth strategies.
1:40–2:15	Summary and evaluation.
2:15–2:30	Closing prayer/benediction.

The Facilitator(s)	Outcome
Two or three different coordinators each session. These persons were also responsible for coordinating the devotional period on Sundays.	This segment empowered the participants because they worked in groups and had the opportunity to learn from one another. Experimentation also was less threatening.
Open to all participants. The pastor or selected minister facilitated the study, but the participants were involved.	We used an action/reflection model (see enclosed information).
Each session, two people would be responsible for setting up coffeepots and sharing one's own or purchased baked goods with the group.	Food and free time are excellent ways to break the ice in group interaction. Plus, more and more persons were involved in helping to shape each vision session.
Facilitated by the pastor or an invited "expert." Much sharing by the group, and their increased leadership of the process.	Through this process, five years of pastoral ministry was framed in my congregation.
Two or three persons from the group.	Two or three persons reflect on what they have learned in the session review. The floor is opened to further questions and direction for the next session.
Groups of two or three people join together in prayer. Concluding prayer said by pastor or group leader.	Important for closure.

- Don't try to handle too many subjects at once.
- As you lead your group in Bible study, give each person an opportunity to express himself or herself. *Don't do all the talking!* Remember, our task is to share the eternal truth of the gospel. People remember more of what is communicated when they contribute to the dialogue.
- As you prepare each session, *try different teaching approaches.* Sometimes you may begin by asking a question. At other times, tell a joke or a story, pass around a picture, or quote poetry or a statement.
- Be alert to the needs of the group. Have persons been missing, had changes in their lives (birth of a baby, robbery or death, an operation)? Can the group and you minister to the person or persons in special need?
- Do the people in your group know one another? Take time during each session for prayer and sharing of stories. Don't just "barge" into Scripture.
- Make certain you have the name, address, and phone number of each person in your group.
- Be aware of a few persons monopolizing the conversation. When questions arise in the group, let the group deal with the question.
- *You are not required to be an answering machine, but rather a facilitator.*

In my New Testament exegesis classes at Union Theological Seminary, Dr. Walter Wink helped his students recognize that Bible study is more than head knowledge or a cognitive exercise.[1] To be most productive Bible study must grab the attention of the reader by reaching the human being in manifold ways: intellectually, emotionally, spiritually, and socially. Interest in the Bible is generated when adult learners are engaged in what is called "action-reflection." This method of Bible study includes learning Bible facts, reflecting on what has been experienced in the unfolding of the story, and determining what we will do in response to reading/experiencing the Word of God. In the study guide at the end of this book, there are listed several other Bible study formats we used in our Vision Group and in our church education programs.

My primary goal in the initial Bible study times was to get our people to come to experience something of the life and ministry of Jesus Christ. This was an important decision because the church is built upon faith in Jesus. The black church is inherently Christological; we are primarily a people with a commitment to Jesus the Christ as our Lord, Savior, Deliverer, and Friend. Black gospel singer Rev. James Cleveland said, "Jesus is the best thing that ever happened to me!"

I selected the Gospel of Mark as our starting point. Mark was selected because it is the earliest Gospel and it is to the point, lacking the literary embellishments of Matthew. It deals with Jesus as spirit-intoxicated, and it is a fabulous lead into the other Synoptic Gospels, the ministry of apostle Paul, and the development of the early church. I provided each participant in the Bible study with the following preparatory tool on Mark to help them gain a sense of the overall thrust of this Gospel witness. Then in our bimonthly meetings, we systematically explored the stories chapter by chapter.

As you read the Gospel of Mark, consider the following:

- Read the Gospel of Mark prayerfully and reverently.
- Use the Revised Standard Version (RSV) as you are teaching/sharing the book.
- Other translations (such as King James Version, Good News, Paraphrased, Jerusalem, and so forth) can and should be consulted.
- Purchase a Bible dictionary and commentary on Mark's Gospel.
- As you read the Scriptures, get a sense of the meaning of each story.
  —Who is in the story?
  —What is each person's role?

—Is there a controversy? a healing? a death?

—Does the story make sense? What are your questions?

- Read each pericope (self-contained story) even if it goes into the next chapter.
- What are the faith issues?
- Do not automatically "side" with Jesus! Try to hear/ feel/taste/touch/see what the other persons are experiencing in the story.
- Where are Jesus' followers in the stories? (In other words, what are their attitudes about Jesus and his ministry?) Where is his family in all this?
- Identify the other story characters and groups. For example, the Sadducees are different from the Herodians. John the Baptist's followers have a different attitude to religion than the Scribes.
- *Don't just know the facts* (who, what, when, where, why and how), but also determine what you feel and know about the story. Is it speaking to you? Does it reach, help, anger, or repel you? Live with the story, don't just experience it in your head. Write down what you are experiencing. How do you feel? What do you see? What issues or questions are raised for you in this story?
- In what way, if any, is the story relevant to your life? home situation? job? church? community?

A systematic reading of Mark's Gospel helped the Vision Group participants understand something of the magnitude, beauty, and challenge of faithful Scripture reading. Participants were continually pressed to determine how the Scripture message could have meaning for their lives. New questions and new interests will emerge as the group continues to study together. After the study of Mark the group wanted to hear more about church leadership, time management, and the use of their talents (see The Study Guide, Sessions 1, 2, and 3).

The Envisioning Process

In an attempt to get New York churches to take their mission seriously, a church training manual titled *Church Development: Answering God's Call,* [2] was submitted to all ABC Metro congregations in 1979. The preliminary design for congregational envisioning was developed years earlier by Rev. Allen Hinand, who shared this instrument with our Vision Group once we were well into our study of Mark's Gospel.

We now also were ready as a group to begin to flesh out a vision for our church. Rev. Hinand reminded us that the first steps in the process were already realized; basic trust was established in the church, a sense of empowerment was taking hold of individual congregants, and the belief that Memorial was not going to die after all was beginning to proliferate. We were on our way. So what to do next? (See The Study Guide, Session 4.)

We held four envisioning sessions. These sessions were undergirded by the notion that our job was to free our imaginations and picture where we wanted our church to be. We looked at our individual pictures and shared these with the group, collectively identifying common images we had of our church.

When adults in the group process are given permission to free their imaginations, incredible floods of possibilities emerge. People begin to see that they are not the only ones to hold a particular view or vision for their church's renewal. A collective picture of the church is conceived. The group then can have an opportunity to become actively involved in determining what forces or factors might contribute to helping or hindering the collective vision of the church.

The Growing Edge: Interpersonal Conflict

After concentrating on the journeys of the individuals who composed the Vision Group and engaging in action/reflection-style Bible study, the participants began to identify problems *within* the congregation that needed attention and correction. We brainstormed and identified fifty or more problems in the church. This is very sensitive business, for once a problem is identified, it is more often than not perceived as caused by some very specific individuals and/or groups. Church people often avoid any possibility of open conflict, especially if it means publicly stepping on the toes of someone that they know may be part of the problem in hindering the forward movement of the church. A skilled enabler[3] (other than the pastor) can be used in order to help the group work through this very painful period of looking at *what* and/or *who* is causing the church to stagnate. Rev. Hinand provided this important service to our group. The objectives were honesty and sincerity.

The Growing Edge

Church people are reluctant to give the impression that they dislike certain people in their congregation. Tremendous possibilities for healing and reconciliation are in evidence when persons are allowed to say how they truly *feel* about another fellow believer or group. Church growth is stunted or stagnated due to underground interpersonal conflicts. Wise leadership allows for periods when the agenda is set aside so that a deepening in relationships is made possible, even if it is accomplished initially through raised voices and angry words! Our church creatively refereed many problems between members as well as destructive power conflicts between competing boards and groups. Two persons in our church had been in conflict for many years. It never was clear to anyone in the congregation what the real dilemma may have been. They simply did not like each other. But their dislike for each other had serious effects on the programs of the church. If one was for a particular new ministry, the other would invariably be against it, no matter how valued this program might be. Each of them had many other supporters who automatically would take their sides.

One of the newer deacons suggested that we confront this

issue head-on. Both persons were asked to come forward and speak to each other. What was happening was that some interpersonal conflicts were beginning to be seen as a shared problem within the Vision Group. As the wall of partition slowly began to fall, the other members circled these two incredible people. We prayed, laughed, and celebrated as they hugged each other for the first time in more than a decade!

To be sure, not every interpersonal conflict in the church is easily overcome. Intentionally ministering to people in conflict will, at a minimum, expose the problem and free the church of the burden of damaging, hidden psychological sabotage by a few irate congregants. These individuals will not always change their behavior quickly or become instantly converted to love the offending or offended other member. Honesty may serve to open up a festering sore. Time may be needed for true healing and reconciliation, but at least healthy honesty and an atmosphere of caring has allowed the hidden problem that retarded the growth of the church to be overcome.

There are many cases when interpersonal conflicts are not easily handled by the pastor or leaders within a congregation. The fact that the conflict has surfaced and seems to be uncontrollable internally should not drive congregational members and leaders to run for cover. Conflict can represent a growing edge or a new breakthrough in the renewing congregation. God's transforming Spirit often causes people to relate to one another in ways different from previous patterns. For example, when honesty becomes a shared ethic of the group, persons who may have avoided or publicly disliked each other will be lovingly confronted. Recalcitrant leaders in decision-making positions often are encountered by people fired with courage to creatively explore new options open to the congregation. But if the resistance to change becomes so entrenched that it cannot be overcome by the internal leadership, it is not an admission of failure to invite your local denominational leadership or a local seminary or university facilitator in to help your congregation cope with its growing pains. These invitees, especially if you use university staff, should have a healthy respect for the church and its mission and should have expertise in enabling groups to learn how to manage conflict.

As I wrote, one issue that our Vision Group decided was a priority was handling our hidden interpersonal conflicts. Once some of the more problematic struggles were honestly and openly confronted, and in large measure resolved, we then were able to focus our attention on two other major issues in our congregation: the orientation and discipling of new members, and the development of organized and sustained outreach ministries in the Central Harlem area. It's hard to tell why these two concerns surfaced as major priorities, especially given the fact that these items took precedence over correcting the terrible physical condition of our church building or the lack of space for class and meeting rooms and administrative offices. More often than not, church committees and groups will decide to repaint, rebuild, or restore their building rather than use its few resources on new members or people in the community. Yet this is what Memorial did!

Let me quickly note here that the church building may be a sacred trust for a congregation. As such, it should be kept as beautiful and clean as possible. Yet we all have seen cases of the "edifice complex" at work in many Christian communities—where the maintenance of the physical building is the primary ministry of that church, with so little attention, time, talent, or treasure deployed for saving, empowering, and enhancing individual persons, families, and communities. What a pity that all too often brick and mortar get in the way of ministry and mission.

I cannot say precisely what triggered the decision at Memorial to focus our attention on developing/orienting new members and engaging in community outreach. It may have been the Bible study lessons on the ministry of Jesus (in Mark) or the discussions which sought to answer the questions, What is the role of the church in today's world? What is a Christian leader? What is my image of my church? that opened the way to lead us in the direction we chose. Another added reality was that many newly affiliated church members had not been a part of church communions before, hence, they were not always overly concerned about the physical appearance of our building. They joined our church because the message finally was breaking through to the outside community that here was a church open to experimenting with new ideas and trying new programs.

I refer here to the discipleship orientation as an "Inreach Strategy," and the community witness (housing work) as an "Outreach Strategy." The following pages tell the story of how these two concerns became central ingredients in the renewal and transformation of Memorial Church. Here's our story.

4

Inreach Strategy:
The Discipleship Process

Confession, we are told, is good for the soul. Hence, my confession.

My ministry at Memorial took place in the midst of six other churches, five of whom are of the same denomination. These churches are all in a less than two-block radius! Our church is the only one literally hidden from view, being located *in* a block; the others are strategically located on avenues.

Within the first two months of my pastorate, seven members of the congregation died. The small, committed circle of believers who remained were understandably disillusioned: a decaying building, inactive or dying membership, limited giving (most members were retired people on fixed incomes), no program ministries, no vision for the future. There was just that little spark waiting for combustion so that a spiritual explosion might take place.

Prayer and the Vision Group made it happen! But from the outset of my pastoral ministry, and in spite of my pain, I was preaching regularly and fervently. Week by week, month by month, scores of people were added to the roll of our church. Within the first two years, 100 people became members of our congregation, and the majority of these were through baptism. These new converts were invited to church by their parents, grandfathers, grandmothers, or next-door neighbors. They were inspired by the presence of the young, new pastor. They witnessed to their relatives and friends, even *in spite* of their ambivalence about my youth, inexperience, and eagerness to change things. Watching our dying church come alive was like Pentecost in Harlem! Still others, who were friends prior to my becoming a pastor, joined. More than fifteen members of my discontinued childhood church also connected with Memorial.

Then it happened. Week by week many came to the church, but just as many left the church who were *not* discipled. It was like catching fish on one side of the boat, and then losing them on the other due to faulty catch basins.

To be honest, I was not in the least bit aware of the crisis. Enough new people dutifully remained to give the appearance that all was well. Their coming on board made a remarkable difference in the ethos of our congregational life; but a hefty majority of the newcomers came a few times to worship, then dropped out of sight. This latter group did not continue in our fellowship, at least partly because we did little or nothing creatively or intentionally to garner their ongoing participation.

This is not to imply that every person who joins a church community will remain if the right conditions exist. But it does mean that if the conditions are right, we may maximize our success in helping more people catch the vision. The problem of my early pastoral years was that I gave little thought to membership beyond the "call-and-response" mechanism that is an important part of most black Protestant (and other) worship experiences.

Beyond the Sunday 11 o'clock hour, there were few support systems to help the newcomer feel welcome, affirmed, and challenged to grow.

In other words, "the right conditions" in our congregation were absent. With this perspective in mind, we can begin to understand why Memorial, and all renewing churches, need a clearly *defined* and enacted discipleship process. In no way is this meant to suggest that this is the one and only way in which one becomes a committed believer. If we were to poll any group of adult Christians, we would find that the molding and shaping influences on their attitudes and loyalties as believers are undoubtedly quite varied. As for me, I had to give serious thought to my own biblical, theological, and pastoral concerns about meeting the needs of the new people, the congregation, and "Outreach," helping them become a vital presence in the Central Harlem community and the world.

Identifying the Problem

Our Vision Group had identified one major problem in our congregation: It possessed poorly trained, inadequately discipled members and leaders. Those who were affected severely by this reality were the new converts. Many of them were inactive and uninvolved in the overall church programs. Many more became "revolving-door saints," connecting with the congregation one week and gone the next.

The Vision Group determined that we needed to develop a viable, coherent strategy of inreach to meet the needs of the new members through intentional training, sharing, fellowship, caring, and personal and group goal setting. The new members were very important indeed—they now represented more than one-half of our church family.

As we became increasingly conscious of the style and form our inreach strategy would take, we began to enact what I call "The Discipleship Process." We still are refining and revamping this program to maximize our chances for success. *Training the newly affiliated people in our congregation became a key method in transforming our church and stabilizing our area of the Harlem community.*

Discipleship: Overcoming Revolving-Door Church Membership

Walter A. Henrichsen's intriguing book, *Disciples Are Made—Not Born,* [1] is "must" reading for every believer. The

Master, Jesus the Christ, challenges his church to make disciples (Matthew 28:19–20).

The making of disciples goes against the grain of most congregations and church leaders. Part of the problem is laziness. It takes time to make a person a committed follower of Jesus Christ.

Another aspect of the problem is the false idea of evangelism that we have witnessed on television or watched in our churches during revival meetings. The call is made to become a Christian. The person comes forward, is voted into membership or signs his or her name to a card or pledge, and that's the end of it. Often the response was forthcoming in the first place because the atmosphere was emotion-packed or pressure-filled by well-meaning family or friends who pushed the candidate forward. But there is no such thing as a "quickie" Christian. A decision for Christ does not inevitably or automatically lead one to become a fully committed believer.

The church machine frequently is its own worst enemy. The need for program funds to keep the building open and pay the bills often forces congregations to solicit new people in fund raising, generally at the expense of their holistic development. This is not to say that saving buildings and maintaining budgets are not worthy endeavors. We can save the whole church building, to paraphrase Jesus, and lose the parishoners' souls.

Another way the misconception arises about this whole discipleship issue is when we read the Gospels without reading between the lines. This is unfortunate. As we watch our Lord move from town to town, from village to village, he is teaching, healing, preaching, and liberating, all of which is leading men, women, and children to understand who they are as loved creations of God. The many stories of persons coming to Christ more often than not are summarizations of what actually took place. Jesus took time with people. Much of the intervening conversations and pauses (also part of the communication process) have been, we can be certain, omitted from the stories handed down to us.

How often many well-meaning Christians try to do a "Jesus number" as they attempt to summon an individual to accept Christ as quickly as possible. Like a bulldozer, they break into a person's well-fortified life and seek his or her surrender—pronto!

True, the urgency of the kingdom call ought to be present in and through all that we say and do, both in our verbal and nonverbal communications; but the manner and method ought to be considered carefully before we bulldoze people out of hell.

Repent!

Jesus was urgent in his appeal. "Repent," he would cry, "for the kingdom of Heaven is at hand" (Matthew 4:17). Such a call was radical and uncompromising. Yet the call to repentance was both a turning *from* and a turning *to*. To "repent" means that one is called *from* a world of inauthenticity, a world of brokenness, a world of sin. Through Jesus one is summoned to a new life—one's authentic existence (John 3:3). One is no longer in the prison house of despair, but is now a recipient of divine grace, unearned and also free of charge.

Yet the call from here to there is a response of the individual to the urgent NOW. It is an invitation to that individual to embark on a costly, continuous spiritual journey both today and tomorrow.

As Walter Henrichsen makes clear, this is precisely the problem with much evangelistic activity. The call of the person *from* is too frequently not followed up by the invitation to *become* (Romans 12:1–8).

Witnessing or evangelism is the beginning stage in a growing process to engage persons in commitment to Christ. To repeat: witnessing is a beginning. On the other hand, *discipleship* is *the ongoing process of what already has begun in Christ through the power of the Holy Spirit and through the agency of clumsy, often inept representatives of God.*

My congregation's plan or strategy of congregational in-reach included orienting and developing new believers in kingdom work and witness. The following represents something of the journey that I travel together with each believer in the new members' class.

The Discipleship Process: The Call

The community of faith should be intentional about and committed to the growth of new believers. Each congregation must assess its own program of discipleship to determine if it is effective, reliable, and relevant given the commands of the Scriptures and the demands of our present historical period. Strange as it seems, many faith communities are content to continue to ignore the new convert or to let the person find his or her own way through the storms of life and the maze of the church, as I was prone to do.

The consequences of our lack of interest or sensitivity to new people are obvious and disastrous. Those who don't catch on to what is going on in the church leave. Those who remain often join the ranks of those generations of pew-sitters and passive pietists. These have been "called out of darkness in the haunting light of inactivity." Many a church calls persons to "come and vegetate." Others call, "come and become a 'busy bee.' "

If our congregational life will be qualitatively different, if we will contribute to the growth of vibrant, committed, and active "change agents" in this day and age, then we must change our thinking about the church's role in preparing people for the work of kingdom building.

The discipleship process begins the moment the unbeliever or Christian feels a sense of a "call." The call comes from God but is more often than not communicated through other human beings. In an adult workshop on repentance, I inquired who was responsible for leading the fifteen participants to Christ. Was it God speaking directly to them, or was it another relative, friend, or stranger? None said it was a direct result of a call from God. Three or four said it was in response to a minister. The bulk of the workshop participants said their calling to salvation was the fruit of the patient work of parents, grandparents, church school teachers, or next-door Christian neighbors and friends. I do not know if these findings ring true in most cases of Christian salvation, but the human connections or the interest shown to the nonbeliever by relatives, friends, and church members is a remarkable magnet of attraction to Christ.

Our calling is both from here to there, as we have said. It is a calling from guilt to grace; from self-hate to self-love; from antisocial behavior to positive social interaction; from fragmented self-identity to wholeness of body, mind, and spirit. The calling is from the world into the kingdom of God. It is discontinuing one's allegiance with the things of this world and their false allurements, and aligning oneself with the Creator and the plan of grace (see Mark 1:15, Romans 8–17).

Persons such as Timothy, who was born into a Christian home, enter the kingdom as a *gradual process.* Others, such as Apostle Paul, experience an almost instant change in their lives. But the entrance into God's kingdom is authentic and genuine when one seeks forgiveness for a life that has majored in self-destruction and minored in communal tenderness and caring for others; when the racist repents of her or his racism; when the sexist repents of his or her sexism; when the oppressed repent of their ongoing sense of powerlessness and the oppressors repent of their obsessive use of power to keep other individuals and sometimes entire communities "in their place." One enters the kingdom after one has said no to the old life and yes to God and God's will for his or her very existence.

The repentance issued is a critical part of discipleship precisely because of one's confession of participation in the conspiracy against God and God's loving plan for creation.

An individual opens oneself to an important truth: I am responsible for much of what is wrong with this world. I no longer can project blame primarily on others. "All have sinned," Paul asserts, "and fall short of the glory of God" (Romans 3:23). The "all" includes me in my personal life and in my role as participant in the organizations and communities where I study, work, recreate, socialize, and sleep.

In the New Testament understanding, repent does not mean a weakly stated "I'm sorry." It is a thorough conviction that my reality as a person and as a community participant is wrong. In Greek, the word for repentance is *metanoia.* It is an about-face, a full change of my "once-was." I stand before God in all my transparency. I admit my public and private sins, those done and those left undone. I confess how I have scandalized God's fabulous creation by my tendency to be hideously hedonistic, selfish, and self-seeking.

As we stand before God and reflect our honest sorrow for what we have done, the Lord, who is our Maker, responds. God is not forced to respond, nor are we deserving of a response. It is a fact of grace, what the older preachers called "the unmerited favor of God." We do not earn grace, nor do we have a right to insist on God's loving forgiveness of our sins.

So often pew and pulpit alike are populated by the unrepentant. The need for repentance comes when we realize our radical need for God, for divine direction, intervention, and benediction in our own lives. Such is the preparation for the coming of the Spirit. The very fact of our renunciation of the old order and antiquated oppressive lifestyles and behavior leads us to become change agents with God—"divine revolutionaries," if you will—filled by the Spirit, and committed to justice, peace, and wholeness for ourselves, our church, our communities, and for the people of the world. That is discipleship preparation at its best. That is what our congregation *had* to affirm through prayer services, worship experiences, Bible study, new member's classes, and in private counseling; the need for recently connected members to take seriously their call to a life of repentance and change.

Baptism: Ordination and Coronation

Careful preparation for baptism also is an important part of the discipleship process. Yet the whole point of its spiritual lesson can be lost if we casually or hastily expose people to the ritual. Baptism is an act of obedience. It is a sign and seal of our commitment to the kingdom of God. As a Baptist by tradition, I feel that immersion in water (where possible) is the best representation of this ritual of induction into the kingdom. I say "best" advisedly. The exclusion or designation of other methods of baptism such as sprinkling or physical anointing is not meant here.

Yet to hear Paul tell it in Romans 6:1–11, the ritual of baptism is a symbol of death and resurrection. This is important for the repentant believer to realize. As one exposes himself or herself to a forgiving God, one must be willing, as Jesus himself was, to be crucified. For the new convert the death is not so much physical as spiritual. The old self is killed. In water baptism the going down into the water is a symbol of our death to old values, lifestyles, attitudes, and behavior patterns. The coming up out of the water represents a type of resurrection of our Lord. As he triumphed over sin, death, and the grave, so we reenact his resurrection as we exit the watery cemetery. That is why we now can "walk in newness of life" (Romans 6:4). It is because, symbolically and actually, we have been given a new lease on life (2 Corinthians 5:17).

Such a baptism is our ordination and coronation. We are set apart for a special work that no one else can do for us—that is *ordination.* In addition, we are given a new understanding of our relationship to God, other persons, and ourselves as "children of the King of kings"—that is *coronation.* For persons whose egos have been viciously bruised by an environment of self-hate and communal negation, what a relief it is to patiently explain what baptism means for their lives.

My pastorate was in need of a maturing vision. I needed to take time through study, private consultation, and prayer to assist each person who responded to the call of God to gain insight into the importance of the ritual of baptism. They needed to know that they are called to responsible "sonship" or "daughtership." They are brought into Christian communion and community not as passive participants, but as vibrant and vital persons who recognize (perhaps vaguely at first) that they have special work to do in furthering the kingdom cause of Jesus Christ. Baptism is the call to come and "grow in grace" (2 Peter 3:18).

Another side of the baptism ritual is the public dimension. There should be no such thing (except perhaps in the case of a dying person) as a private baptism. That is because there is no such thing as private Christianity. The creation of so great a cloud of uninvolved pious individualists over the centuries is, at least in part, an outgrowth of a privatistic notion of baptism that states that we are saved from ourselves, for ourselves. How tragic! The truth is, until the emphasis is made on the baptism ritual as a call to affirm one's connection and responsibility to community and other structures, organizations, and institutions—most especially the church—we are in danger of continuing in many congregations an attitude of disinterest and uncaring about such "mundane" concerns as voter registration, tutoring youth, volunteering for scout leadership, visiting the sick, restoring housing, seeking to change unjust laws, and other outreach possibilities.

My inactive congregation was not about to suddenly come alive out of the blue. As new people joined, there was no reason on earth why they should become involved in church and community concerns unless the emphasis of their initial training had focused on what it meant to be called and baptized in the first place.

Second, so many stereotypes abound related to the baptism ritual, not the least of which is fear that the minister may drown them. Along with the deacons and church school, youth, and adult leaders, clarification of the meaning of baptism began to open new people (and some of the old-timers) to what it means to say "I accept Jesus Christ as my Savior." The inreach strategy began to help new members discover the rich meaning of the symbols of faith. It also led them to appreciate and accept the meaning of grace—God's choosing, calling, and converting them—for the ministry of sharing and caring through their church, into the communities where they live, play, socialize, worship, or work.

Baptism: The Public Dimension

The new convert also needs to discover that there is a reciprocal aspect to baptism as well. Just as the new convert is baptized in public to emphasize one's responsibility and privilege in the community of faith, so the congregation also is present to bear witness to their commitment to the growth and development of the new believer.

In Jesus' late-night interview with Nicodemus, as recorded in John 3:3–7, the Lord makes clear that one cannot enter the kingdom unless one is born again. One is born the first time inside the mother's womb, then one is born the second time within the womb of the body of baptized believers. This body is the *ekklesia* or the church. Just as one has a birthday, so one also has a "spiritual birthday."

Our congregation began to intentionally hold our baptism on important holidays, such as the night of Maundy Thursday or Easter, but mostly before or after a designated Sunday service prior to the first Sunday Lord's Supper. This is done to maximize the chances of full congregational participation. The baptism services are viewed as important celebrations. There is always singing, explanation of the baptism rite, and a post-baptism charge to the congregation to not only care for and nurture the new believer, but also to seek to win others to Christ.

Church Support Systems: Spiritual Brothers and Sisters

As one joins our congregation, that person is given *spiritual brothers or sisters.* These persons, roughly of the same age as the convert, befriend the newcomer and enable greater integration into the life of the fellowship. Other congregations have a prayer partner or a designated mature Christian to enable the new believer. In addition, the member is assigned to a new member's class. She or he becomes exposed to the ministry of the church and the basics of spiritual life development, including an introduction to the Bible, how to pray, how to manage one's money and time, how to receive the Holy Spirit into one's life, and how to discover and use one's gifts in the support of the cause of the extended family in the community and the world. (See The Study Guide, Sessions 2 and 3 for examples of this type of study. This also was the system of study for Vision Group members.)

Minisermon Inserts

Communications in the form of "minisermons" from my desk are included in the weekly church bulletins. Many are left in the pews, unread. But every now and then, some stalwart soul approaches me with refreshing words: "Your insert really reached me this week!" I try my best to improve on these by having selected groups, such as the officers, ministers, or church school enablers, read them aloud. I can tell by the way they read how much I am communicating clearly. Besides, a sixteen-year-old gentleman dared approach this seminary-trained minister to help me write more effectively! Parish life can humble the best of us!

Included here is one sample of a bulletin insert I wrote entitled, "An Autopsy of a Dead Church." Needless to say, the title alone of this minisermon was greeted with unusual attention.

The coroners of the spirit are crowding in on the decaying corpse of a dead church. Their principal concern is to determine why this church died. They take the corpse apart, and though the diagnosis is not conclusive, the preliminary report suggests that the church died of spiritual malnutrition. Or to put it in laymen's language: the church died from starvation of its spiritual life.

Let's see what might have happened. . . .

Stale and Cold Worship

The people who came to this now-dead church were not turned on by the corporate worship. The Sunday 11 A.M. hour was humdrum, lacking in interest. In fact, there seemed to be no spark. No zap. No real vibrant praise or sense of celebration that would put the congregants in touch with God, with one another, and with their community. Sunday worship was stale, lifeless, boring, and predictable.

The congregational singing had been reduced to whispering praise. The singing from the hymnbook was joyless, and the musicians seemed to move their fingers over the ivory keys, but their hearts and minds had drifted into another world. During the services the pew-sitters seemed preoccupied with passing notes and showing their recent photos, not in centering their minds on the proper object of worship: CHRIST.

The preaching hour seemed to reach no one. It always was the same sermon on the usual themes: love, hope, faith, and so forth, but spoken without conviction from "the sacred desk." Mere words dangled like skeletons before the people; they lacked skin on the bone. After the morning worship one could see the members rush for the doors as if the building was on fire! That church, to use Hollis L. Green's words, had "lost its Sunday punch!" For that matter, it had lost its reason to be the church.

Unloving Fellowship

The church died, not only because of its disconnected worship, but also because there was a noticeable absence of commitment of the members toward one another. The few new members—if any happened to come through the doors—were treated as fund raisers, not as colleagues together in Christ. No one could care in the least about their spiritual growth or nurture. In fact, few of the old-timers concerned themselves with finding out what the new members' names were. The fellowship of this now-dead church was virtually nonexistent, for there was an absence of a common concern for one another among the flock. A lack of friendship and friendliness killed this church.

Stingy Giving

What a church it was! Financial support for the church's programs came from a handful of the members. They ran fund-raising events and gave of their money unselfishly. Yet it appears that the mass of the members felt that it was their sacred duty to place in the plate one George Washington. Now by all calculations, their dollar was burned up by oil or electrical usage even before they put it in the offering receptacle. Year after year, the church had to cut back its services and programs because the members refused to sacrifice to support their church. So it died.

A Limping Church School

What possibilities there were for this church to live had it been fed intravenously through ongoing Christian education and nurture. But only a few stalwart souls attended church school—a tiny minority. This remnant came to understand the Scriptures more fully and the meaning of Christ-centered living more deeply.

The bulk of the congregation withered away spiritually because they were not feeding on the life-giving bread of

God's Word. What a pity! So the church school limped along, as the defenseless members one by one were ambushed by the devil.

A Faithless People

As the church was sighing its last breath, members of the church became increasingly discouraged. They began to feel a sense of hopelessness and disinterest in the ongoing work of ministry throughout their congregation. They could see only the deteriorating circumstances. Lacking the faith to seize the time and become more involved in the life of the congregation and community, they prepared themselves for the inevitable demise of their church.

A Crisis of Christlessness

The coroners of the spirit stared at the decaying corpse of the dead church and concluded that its principal medical malady was the fact that the people of the congregation suffered from a crisis of Christlessness. Some were religious. A few were faithful. But all too many of the members lacked a commitment to Jesus Christ. The church suffered from an absence of Christ-centeredness.

A Christian church can be a dead church—a church that flounders because there are no spiritual roots, no driving concern to win persons for Jesus Christ. There is lacking a desire to have a face-to-face encounter with the Man from Nazareth—God's only begotten Son. Men and women, individuals and families without Christ are without meaning, purpose, and direction.

In our modern, technocratic world, the coroners of the Spirit are busy seeking to determine why so many congregations are dying. But Jesus calls out to dying churches and decaying Christians. He says, "I came that [you] may have life, and have it abundantly" (John 10:10). A church that is willing to turn from the lifeless routine of sameness and routine-unto-death to a vibrant Christ is a church that will live, grow, and prosper to the glory of God!

The Wilderness

One of the most challenging aspects of urban ministry is to help people see that there is a "wilderness"—a place of testing—waiting for every believer (Mark 1:12–13). This call to the wilderness is more than a holy seduction or allurement. Mark's Gospel goes so far as to call it an occasion of unavoidable "drivenness." We are, as Jesus, "driven" into the wilderness. When we get there (wherever *our* wilderness happens to be), our very understanding of the meaning of baptism is not only questioned but also severely—sometimes devastatingly—challenged.

There are so many heavy burdens that accompany our metropolitan trek. To speak of adding to the everyday sense of burdens, God's burdens, God's testing of our very identity, borders on heresy. Yet until each urban church helps persons come to understand the costliness of God's grace, then we become nothing more than a society of pew-sitters and passive pietists, refusing to respond to the needs on the city pavement.[2] This is where our Lord is calling us, testing us, burdening us. This is where most churches refuse to lead people, to drive people.

If nothing else, wilderness helps us develop a deepening sense of *who* we are as God's anointed because we can no longer rely upon *what* we are as our divine identity unravels. No matter what one's social position, race, language, church affiliation, family background; anyone who rides the New York subways, for instance, is *ipso facto* stripped of any possible pretenses. How often has it been said during a tussle at rush hour, "Hey, if you don't like the pushin', use your limousine!"

After a Sunday morning baptism, riding a subway on Monday morning can be just like being driven into the wilderness. Do we smile as others push? Do we push and shove back now that we've come to a new understanding of our relationship with God? Do we wait until everyone else gets to work, and arrive late just so we won't get ugly? Such

decision making may sound trivial but it is not. One sobering fact of the urban Christian's calling is the Monday
morning subway or bus ride. The question of how one lives
out the new faith in relation to anonymous subway push-
ers/shovers; uncaring next-door neighbors; gossiping, competitive co-workers; or unsuccessful relationships is a call to
meet life's temptations not in a monastery or sequestered
church building but in the wilderness called metropolis.

Helping believers triumph in the wilderness is a tangible
though difficult objective of the discipleship process. In our
congregation men and women who were overloaded by their
share of pain and problems still sing:

"Tell me how did you feel when you come out the wilderness, leaning on the Lord?"[3]

Incarnational Christianity

How can the gospel become relevant and liveable in the
urban wilderness? I suspect that the theology of the incarnation makes a great deal of sense for the believer who
must survive in the absurd arena of daily living called the
city. The incarnation is represented by our Lord, who left
the realms of eternity and perfection and dared enter the
tug-and-pull of our day-to-day world. The notion of incarnation, in my opinion, is a real "drag" if *all* Jesus could
expect of his incorporation of eternal into human reality
was drudgery, strife, and death. True, he knew that the
plan of salvation would lead to death on the cross. Calvary
is our sober reality of the costliness of discipleship, the call
of commitment, and the challenge of involvement.

But there's much more. Did not Jesus of Nazareth spend
time sharing stories, meeting new people, enjoying the prepared meals of delighted hosts? Did he not laugh, make
merry, and discover (from God's side) that the human enterprise was not hopeless or devoid of winsome, loving possibilities? Is that not part of the reason why God loves the
world, because Jesus discovered deep insights into this

human unfolding? Perhaps he "reminded" God that the creation with which the Creator labored, is, after all, worth saving.

As we enter the wilderness with the perspective of incarnation, our presence in the world also ought reflect a refreshing attitude about the created order in which we live. As believers, the discipleship process might well resist a them/us attitude that leads us to falsely believe that we are better, or more holy, or of a different breed than the rest of God's creation. Maybe we should accept the fact that we are sinners saved by grace. Grace is a free gift of God. We could not earn it. We did not deserve it. But God loved us so much that "God looked beyond our faults and saw our needs"[4]: the *need* for our holistic, total salvation and liberation.

As we incarnate ourselves in the work of the kingdom, we have a story to tell about the exciting, amazing grace of God. Yes, we earnestly seek to live rightly and attuned to God's will. As the Lord's Prayer puts it: "Thy will be done, on earth as it is in heaven" (Matthew 6:10). Our families, jobs, schools, churches, social connections, institutions—in short, the arenas of our wilderness—call us to let our light shine to spread the Good News that the kingdom of God is at hand, to be vulnerable enough to recognize that we are seeking God's way even as we lead others to discover it. Neither the new convert nor the seasoned saint need put on airs about being "better" than other persons in the city. We need only be humble—fully *human.* We can be God's people who affirm and seek to share with others what the Lord of life intends for both the city and the world: the realization of the kingdom of God!

Of course, I could not "throw" this at new people all at once. But my sensitivity to their need to understand what they were *doing* by joining our church made me search out a greater understanding of how we might reach and keep them.

Revitalizing Worship: Sharing the Word

Church-growth people are in the clutch of a great debate of whether public preaching makes much of a difference in congregational renewal or in the growth in the number of converts. I've tossed this issue around in my mind a lot. If I thought in the slightest way that I've really delivered the Word—at least in the way the New York pulpit giants such as my mentor and former pastor, Gardner C. Taylor, William Augustus Jones, or the late Sandy F. Ray do—then I guess I have begun to preach! But week by week, as I check the pulse of my fellow preachers/pastors and glimpse their insights and novel ways of retelling the grand old story, I realize how much more growing and maturing I have to do.

Yet every now and then, the thought invades my consciousness. In the first place God must have known what God was doing in calling Preston Robert Washington to preach the gospel, even if Rev. Washington has not always been exactly certain. Second, the people in my congregation are not listening and responding to another preacher/pastor. Their choice is to hear and dialogue with me! Such a sublime privilege is not only paradoxical, but also downright frightening. Like any other preacher, the amazing grace that I have experienced is when I have gone home with head bowed, feeling deep in my heart that I have failed and failed miserably. Then a mother will call and say something like "Pastor, you spoke to me this morning! I was burdened and tired. You gave me strength to keep on going."

The point of preaching's importance is to be understood in the context of the powerful Word of God, empowering both pulpit and pew to become change agents in the community and the world.

Hearing the Word

Beyond those moments when the minister is privileged to enter the life pulse of another life through preaching, there are other challenging responses coming from the pew. Once the preaching task is understood as *relevant dialogue* rather than theological monologue, many persons are affirmed, cajoled, challenged, embittered. But whatever the emotional or heart response, they are moved from dead-center complacency and lethargy. Energy flows.

The discipleship process also is a matter of enabling persons to really "hear" the Word of God as part and parcel of their own life story. For the black preacher at least, an unpardonable sin in many a congregation is the inability or failure to tell the story.[5] But an equally unpardonable sin of the pew is its failure or refusal to allow the truth of God's will (through the dialogue of preaching) to penetrate the earlobes and filter into the brain. Most of us are, generally speaking, spiritually hard of hearing. If we are not altogether deafened to God's voice, we often engage in selective tuning—snatching only those things that are, more often than not, palatable or pleasurable. The preacher/prophet must at times speak in thunderous judgment, upsetting the calm seas of our daily lives. When she or he does, the believer must come to see, assuming the sincere and deliberate life-altering concern of God's messenger, that this is the Word of life, even if it sometimes hurts. Indeed, if the teaching to really hear preaching is part of the believer's course in spiritual growth (however informal this may be), congregations begin to "yearn" to hear and share God's Word of truth. A biological tuning mechanism comes into operation in each believer's life so that if the preaching transaction is not humdrum, lackluster, or one-sided, there is no mass exiting to the rest room or baby-cooing during the entire discourse.

The messenger also must help to make the preaching hour God's shining encounter with both himself or herself, as well as with the rest of the congregation. Obviously, we are not always at our best, but neither do we dare parade our shoddy, ill-prepared homilies before the people entrusted to us. God forbid we unwittingly contribute to the reduced readiness of the flock to hear what God has to say through our already stuttering tongues.

Hearing and Sharing the Word

One way the discipleship process contributed to Memorial's heightened regard for hearing preaching is when the people were asked to bring and open their Bibles during worship. The text and context of the delivery is now a shared encounter rather than a one-way quote coming from the messenger's desk. This also helped persons to really open their Bibles, perhaps (and we hope this is not often true) for the only time during the week. The enriched living that proceeds from sharing in the biblical unfolding is unmeasurable. The more opportunities afforded laypersons and auxiliary clergy to share their stories in the light of God's Word, the greater the congregational regard for the message and the messenger.

Lay members of our congregation preach "The Seven Last Words" of Christ from the cross each Good Friday evening. I have been amazed at the many-splendored ways these sensitive souls have written and presented quite challenging and enriching homilies. Some congregations also have "platform services" where several laypersons preach a minisermon on a particular subject. For example, seven persons might be selected to preach a five-minute message on one of the churches of Asia Minor found in Revelation chapters 1 to 3. At the conclusion of these services, a minister or lay congregant might challenge the hearers to determine which type of church they represent. Discussion can be a vital part of this experience as those present may break up into small groups to look at ways of understanding some of the problems and possibilities of the early Christian communities.

Finally, we discovered that at the heart of the discipleship process there must be a conscious attempt to give new believers and the faithfully committed long-standing members a challenge. They must bear and share the kingdom of God with the world. This process begins by gifting new and old leaders.

Gifting New and Old Leaders

When the church invites an individual or family to "come grow," there ought to be viable options for the personal/ communal development of each believer.

I am intrigued and fascinated by the many churches and denominations that presently are helping laity identify and use gifts of the Spirit. Such Scriptures as Romans 12, 1 Corinthians 12, and Ephesians 4 are employed to buttress this most encouraging new development in contemporary Christianity. We begin to identify this need for gift identification by focusing on the neglected pew.

"Lay lib!" has been a vital ingredient in my own church's renewal, as we have intentionally solicited the involvement of larger and larger numbers of inactive church attendees. More and more persons have initiated ministries of healing of the physically and mentally ill (for both individuals are known to our church or in it). The numbers of members engaging in the teaching and preaching ministries have been breathtaking, especially considering the tiny church school we inherited. A lay-witnessing core group has shown impressive beginnings, and a committed segment of the congregation has sought to live out an evangelistic lifestyle. One group initiated an outreach ministry in the nearby housing complex. Another group developed contact with a "last stop" correctional facility (inmates are there for thirty-to-sixty days before parole). Still another group of members aligned themselves to a ministry of housing stabilization, as our congregation sought and continues to seek to become incarnationally present in the lives of our next-door neighbors. Indeed, a small circle of believers within the church have even developed a sharing ministry with jazz artists, poets, dancers, and singers. Much of this activity is informal. Yet the recent avalanche of activist ministry by our members is a far cry from a few years ago, when none of this activity took place. Why then was there an almost overnight explosion?

Perhaps part of the explanation might be attributed to what has evolved as the stance that the official boards and I have taken: We have become *spiritually permissive!* Once we let go of petty fund raising, other counterproductive programming (in the name of survival), and interpersonal conflicts and power plays, people were free to begin to use their energy (that had previously been employed in candy sales, confrontations, and ticket-selling) for the doing of ministry.

While reviewing old sermons from my teenage years, it was amazing how much of a child of the 1960s I was. Almost all of my messages made some reference to challenging people to "go out" and "do" something. Had one of the sixty- or seventy-year-old listeners come to me and asked, "Do what?" I probably would have been hard-pressed to give a clear reply. I still am. In spite of the impressive rise of activism in my present congregation, many members are still inactive. Yet those who are involved have basically acted on a spiritual hunch.

1. They are involved with activities and people they care about.
2. They feel more-or-less comfortable with the fact that this (whatever the activity is) is what they can do best.
3. They feel free to pursue their ministries because no one is looking over their shoulders to condemn them or put a halt to their creativity.

Later we shall discuss in more detail some implications for church renewal as we explore one aspect of our outreach work: housing stabilization of our buildings next door to the church. Clearly then, the discipleship process also must include the identification and utilization of gifts of people who may never have believed they even had them. These discovered gifts are valuable for the sharing and doing of ministry in the broader community.

1. The discipleship process helped the new members (and many long-standing ones as well) understand more fully the call of God in their lives; their baptism; the preparation for hearing, reading, and doing the Word; the fellowship with their spiritual brothers and sisters; and their progressive identification of their gifts for doing practical ministries. This created a new vitality in our congregation's life. We all have been enriched and enlivened by the newer members and strengthened and stabilized by the older members. We opened ourselves in prayer and sought every available opportunity to dialogue.

2. As the church is opened up to the new vision by God, newer people are able and willing to become leaders. Their attitudes and feelings are induced by the notion of growth, change, and renewal as a positive, welcomed process. The Vision Group stimulated the transformation process, leading us to finally take seriously the vital presence of new believers.

3. The transformation of the Spirit—renewal, growth, and development—cannot remain a congregational affair alone. Once persons who are encountered by the Christ become aligned with the Lord of life, and earnestly desire opportunities to worship, celebrate, learn, and share, the inreach strategies or the discipleship process frequently lead to work and witness outside the four walls of the local church. To be sure, the discipleship process does not end, for as new persons join the company of the redeemed, they need the same if not an improved discipleship process. Transformation is realized when many people reach out to transform their communities, homes, and schools or the homes of their neighbors.

Memorial is no exception. As stated before, we have enacted many formal and informal mission programs and projects in our community in health, evangelism, artistic expression, family ministries, prison outreach, and home Bible study. We isolate for this discussion, however, one major area of our congregation's present outreach strategy: housing stabilization.

5

Outreach Strategy: Housing Ministries

The Vision Group had noted that one organizational barrier in our church was that we had few organized, sustained outreach ministries in the Lower Harlem area (see The Study Guide, Session 5).

For the life of me, I cannot understand what the prayer versus social action and Bible study versus community service debate is about. The best in black Christian faith knows no distinction or contradiction between the gospel and the development of caring ministries. Sociological reality dictates a *holistic gospel.*

If not even affluent congregations can enjoy the luxury of noninvolvement in the marketplaces of life, how can the black church do it? *Any* church that refuses to address the basic needs of people, whether they are the concerns of kids in a well-to-do suburb who feel unloved, or kids in Harlem who cannot find employment, is not much more than a social club or a "society" of Jesus Christ. We would have to stretch our imaginations to call it church—God's school of spiritual transformation. At this present time that black church has been forced to enter the debate between the pietists and the activists and to declare, "Let's have both!"

At any rate, Memorial *had* to address some of the issues in our community. We had no choice.

At the point in which I assumed the pastorate of Memorial, Harlem was (and still is) up for grabs. Greed destroys the community. Uncaring real estate speculators had, for the past fifty years, bled the community dry by skimming profits off the top of the rent rolls and reinvesting precious few dollars into building maintenance and repairs. The result was radically deteriorated housing stock; overcrowded and inadequate (and often inhuman) living conditions; and a resulting atmosphere of psychological, spiritual, and social depression and despair.

Memorial *had* to address the issue of inadequate housing for families and the resulting closing out of the small commercial concerns. Again, one major outreach strategy our congregation initiated was housing education of our members, tenant organizing, building ownership, maintenance, management, and renovation. In short, we worked toward *housing and community stabilization.* Some questions might be raised, such as Why and how did Memorial get involved in housing work?

The Road to Housing and Community Stabilization

Sociological Issues: The Harlem Challenge

Memorial is located in Central Harlem. We are located just five blocks north of Central Park. The Harlem Community[1] is an area consisting of 3,829 acres. Its northern boundary is 178th Street and its southern boundary is 96th Street. The east-west borders are the East and Harlem Rivers (east), and the Hudson River (west). There are approximately 122 persons per acre. Blacks in Harlem constitute 49 percent of the population; whites, 14 percent; Hispanics, 34 percent; Asians, 1.43 percent; and others, 1.35 percent. It should be noted that the largest concentration of blacks can be found in Central Harlem and West

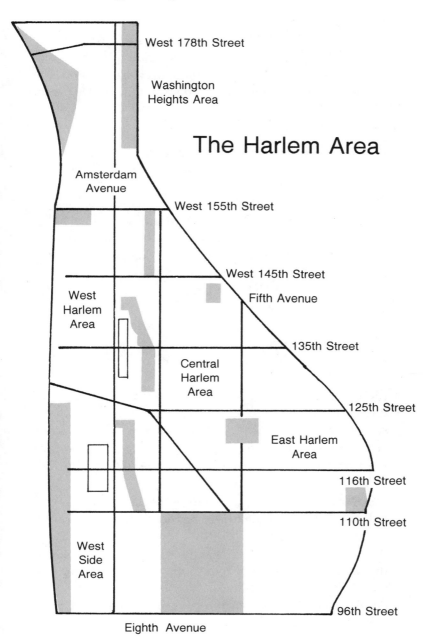

West 178th Street

Washington
Heights Area

The Harlem Area

Amsterdam
Avenue

West 155th Street

West 145th Street

Fifth Avenue

West
Harlem
Area

135th Street

Central
Harlem
Area

125th Street

East Harlem
Area

116th Street

110th Street

West
Side
Area

96th Street

Eighth Avenue

Harlem, and the largest concentration of Hispanics is located in East Harlem. The white and Asian constituents are located south of 110th Street, especially in the West Side. There are 175,515 households in Harlem, and the most recent figure (1986) on unemployment is 18.1 percent.

In the community of Harlem, there are:

- high crime, drug-trafficking and addiction rates
- deteriorated and below-standard housing (much of which is government subsidized)
- large numbers of elderly persons on fixed incomes
- increased cases of white police violence against black and Hispanic community residents (the police often are perceived as an "occupation force" keeping the "colony" in check)
- few small- or modest-size legitimate businesses under the control of local residents
- limited manufacturing, communication, transportation, and financial institutions to provide employment and/or investment opportunities for area residents
- thousands of teenagers and young adults who are unemployed (estimated at 50–75 percent), or who have *never* held a job. New York City is known as a disaster area for minority teenagers. Black teenagers experience the highest unemployment rate in the nation (*The New York Times,* August 1, 1983)[2]
- thousands of young persons—especially men—who will either die tragic deaths or be incarcerated before the age of twenty-five
- thousands of teenage girls who will give birth before the age of eighteen and live on government entitlements for their entire lives
- public schools that are notorious for continued poor academic performance

- a radical decrease in medical facilities. There is only one public and one private hospital left in Central Harlem to meet the needs of area residents
- *one* movie theater and only limited entertainment options
- no viable hotels or motels.

To be sure, Harlem is a much-studied community. Part of the reason is that it is a prototype, a symbol of oppressed communities across this nation and throughout the Third World. Like all too many areas where minority residents live, Harlem is a place of severe economic depression. Gentrification, redlining by banks and financial institutions, governmental sabotage, unemployment, drugs; and the lack of unified, constructive action on the part of churches, mosques, social agencies, and political groups in the area have all conspired to make this "black capital of the world" a dying community that has lost much of its former glory and vitality.

Europeans and other tourists who have read or heard about Harlem often ask as they meander the streets of this once-thriving community, Is this the place where the Reverends Adam Clayton Powell, Sr. and Jr.; Marcus Garvey; and Malcolm X organized and ministered to countless thousands? Is this the birthplace of the Harlem Renaissance, where cultural geniuses such as Langston Hughes, Claude McKay, and Countee Cullen dared speak with new tongues? Can this possibly be the setting where Claude Brown, James Baldwin, and Nikki Giovanni detonated literary bombshells that shook the white publishing world?" We sadly must respond to our friends: "Yes, this is *that* Harlem."

On the other hand, filthy streets, abandoned buildings, and wasted lives tell only a part of the Harlem story. The economics of oppression and pain are not the only reigning realities in the continuing saga of the near-death of a community. There are healthy signs of a new Harlem Renaissance. •

The New Harlem Renaissance

Harlem is blessed with a sustaining, almost invisible infrastructure of churches, mosques, political clubs, Masonic orders, food and credit cooperatives; banks; economic organizations; social, fraternal and cultural organizations; theaters; and community self-help groups. Harlem is the home of the City College of New York, The Schomberg Center for the Study of Afro-American Life and Culture, the Harlem Studio Museum, the Adam Clayton Powell State Office Building, and Minisink Town House, to name a few of the many institutions. Harlem is vexed by property, but a thriving middle class is housed throughout the community from Schomberg Plaza to Esplanade Gardens, from the brownstones of Strivers Row to Sugar Hill, from Lenox Terrace to Riverbend Houses. The Harlem Urban Development Corporation (HUDC), the Harlem Commonwealth Council, Freedom National Bank, Carver Federal Savings, and other community agencies have done much to foster the slow recovery of the community. There are other numerous vital signs that the community is coming alive again. Public and private housing renovations such as those initiated by St. Phillips Episcopal Church, and the new construction of three major housing projects of Rev. Wyatt Tee Walker's Canaan Baptist Church of Christ are evidences of this rebirth.

The truth is, though Harlem has been assaulted and nearly strangled to death, there have been varied forces of life and empowerment that predated—or emerged simultaneously with—the antipoverty programs of the 1960s. Often these groups, agencies, and individuals have sensed the urgent need to improve, enhance, and empower their corner or area of the Harlem puzzle. In a word, there is an emerging consciousness in Harlem. A refreshing wind is blowing throughout the community. It is a new spirit of redevelopment—unified efforts to foster economic, social, cultural, and political transformation of a community striving to re-gain its place in the sun.

Enter Memorial.

Target: The Mission Field Next Door

Our Vision Group identified housing deterioration in our area as a priority of outreach. As a congregation we had no choice but to either engage in housing stabilization or allow the buildings on either side of our church to go up in flames after their imminent total abandonment. Dr. Wyatt Tee Walker, my colleague in ministry and a pioneer in new housing construction in Harlem, calls the church's involvement in housing work "enlightened self-interest." Indeed, had Memorial refused to open itself to the risks of housing ministry, there might not *be* a church standing in its present location.

The drug addicts and pushers would have seen to that. During the winter, they huddled around a burning trash basket in the hallway of 100 St. Nicholas Avenue in order to keep warm. The boiler of the building had burned out, hence, frozen pipes burst throughout the housing complex, forcing the remaining few families to use the hydrant outside in order to get water for sanitation, cooking, and bathing. Even though less than one-fourth of the thirty-three apartments were inhabited, there were over thirty children and youth remaining in 100, not including scores of adults with no place to go.

The landlord had taken his profits out of the limited rent roll but did absolutely nothing to maintain the building or provide basic services to the remaining apartment dwellers. After little profit could be realized from this near-abandoned building, the owner essentially abandoned ship. The commercial renters attempted to organize a tenants' association and pool rent in order to generate sufficient revenue to provide heat, hot water, and minimal building care. But tenants who have lived with dishonest landlords and criminally neglectful housing managers are not likely to quickly trust a new regime, no matter how well intentioned those persons happen to be.

It was the twilight zone for 100. Dope-addicted youth and drug-dispensing adults thrust the building and the neighborhood into chaos. The building itself suffered through all too many winters of despair, leaving bursting pipes to flood entire apartments. Tenants were forced to light gas kitchen stoves in order to keep warm, thereby creating a dangerous possibility of exposing families to carbon monoxide poisoning. The walls of the apartments had been painted with lead-based paints, and several tots became ill from eating the chips and peelings. Indeed, I conducted three funerals for tenants who had died of pneumonia in this building.

So our church was not confronted by problems of groups struggling to survive in some distant mission field. The issue of ministry was right next door, a stone's throw away from our church. There were radical needs to be met in 100: persons suffering from a slumlord's insensitivity and greed, a distrust of the tenants within the house, and lawlessness in the hallways and adjacent streets surrounding the building.

The death of a community happens when building after building is thrust into financial chaos. On the other side of the church structure, another house, 135 West 115th Street, had become an "interim lease" building. This means that the landlord either abandoned the building or was forced to lose ownership because he could not afford to pay city real estate taxes while also providing heat, maintenance, and superintendent needs to the building. Usually, landlord abandonment results from the low rents that do not cover inflationary prices. Hence, 135 became another housing casualty in New York.

Memorial was confronted by a crisis. Buildings on either side of the church were in severe financial and physical condition. The tenants were thrust into the unenviable position of not knowing from day to day if they would lose their homes because of arson, suffer an overtaking of their buildings by drug addicts and pushers, or be forced to leave because the city had limited, inadequate public funds to maintain their buildings.

Technical Assistance

Christians do not believe in chance. It could not be by accident that just at the time Memorial Church was confronted by the reality of the severe plight of 100 and 135, the American Baptist Churches of Metropolitan New York and its executive minister, Rev. Carl E. Flemister, had hired Rev. Donald W. Morlan to serve as their public mission staff member with principal responsibility to assist local churches in developing housing ministries.

Don had served as pastor of the Chambers Memorial Baptist Church in East Harlem, where he had been responsible for developing three million dollars for housing programs. He came well equipped for this exciting, innovative ministry.

Carl Flemister and the administrative board of ABC Metro New York must be congratulated for the viable support they rendered to struggling congregations like ours as we launched out into the public mission arena.

Long-Term Involvement

Don suggested that if Memorial were to get involved in housing, it would have to be a *churchwide decision.* Without the church's commitment housing programs, like other community outreach projects, can be interpreted as the present pastor's pet interest. Housing involvement requires a congregational investment of twenty-to-forty years or even longer. Most pastors don't last that long in any given church.

The Vision Group set the stage for our congregation's attitudinal change by putting before us the challenge to develop a mission project in Central Harlem. What could be more viable than to help save the homes of our neighbors right next door to our church? Memorial went on record as a congregation committed to long-term housing stabilization in the Lower Harlem neighborhood.[3]

The Power of the Opposition

Don led us in the fight to capture—to own—the 100 building. The slumlord who owned the house wanted to give 100 to the church. Of course, had we accepted this seemingly lucrative offer, we would have given this greedy individual a tax write-off of nearly one million dollars. The church would have inherited the building's hundreds of financial liabilities.

We hired a topflight real estate lawyer (paid for by the Revolving Risk Fund of ABC's National Ministries) and fought for direct ownership of the property by a separately incorporated housing committee consisting of church members. We were able to take this legal route because one of the agencies that had lent the landlord a substantial sum of money was never repaid in full by him. Once they discovered the damage the landlord had done to countless human beings and the commitment of our church to transform our area, they turned the first mortgage over to us.

The battle in the courtroom dragged on for two long years. Not only was this a costly enterprise, but also some of our church members began to question the wisdom of fighting so powerful a real estate battle. Unscrupulous leaders in the community joined with the landlord in condemning our church! They contended that we were inexperienced, poor people who knew nothing about running so large a real estate endeavor as 100. They knew that our ownership of 100 would signal the end to their substantial business in the building.

I do not know who initiated another formidable group— the drug pushers—to come forward and threaten not only my life, but also the health and safety of Mrs. Ruth Browne, our housing worker. Many of my closest church friends strongly urged me to give up the fight and leave 100 alone. I could not. I am a product of Harlem, so I have seen death all about me. To be sure, I was scared nearly to death. But

I just could not give up the fight. Too many families and too many lives were hanging in the balance.

Finally, the news came like dewdrops in the desert: The landlord had lost ownership of 100 and our church housing committee was the new owner. This was no small victory. Harlem, like urban areas across the country, gradually is being *gentrified.* Banks, landlords, and private investors stake out vulnerable areas where mostly poor and lower-middle-class people live and substantially renovate the housing stock or build expensive condominiums, cooperative apartments, and townhouses. The present area residents cannot afford them, so they are forced to search desperately for an apartment within their financial means, which rarely exists. The struggle of the urban poor and the lower-middle-class is to save their homes. Our battle for 100 was one small but incredible victory.

The Human Factors: Organizing the Tenants

As previously stated, I already was pastor to our next-door neighbors from officiating at funerals and writing advocacy letters to receive social service entitlements for financially strangled families. On the other hand, my congregation was *not* involved in the lives of tenants until we called our first series of meetings with the residents of 100 and 135.

The tenant meetings for both buildings always were held separately due to the fact that the internal politics in each building was totally different. There were twenty-one families in 135. These were people who basically had lived in this Harlem apartment house for over twenty-five years, and hence, our mutual goal was to prepare their city-owned building to become a tenant-owned cooperative. A building owned and operated by people who had never co-owned before was quite a challenge!

The story in 100 was altogether different. The building was almost empty. Our housing manager and member, Mrs. Ruth Browne, encouraged many families to move into these humble, previously ill-kept apartments. Most of these people had moved from building to building—some because of arson or eviction because they could not pay the high Harlem rents, others because they could not find affordable apartments in their neighborhoods. Our conviction and mutual goal with these tenants was to seek city housing and bank financing to renovate the building; fix the major systems (heat, electrical, plumbing); repair the broken elevator; restore the roof; and provide more viable living quarters for families in these huge five-, six-, and seven-room apartments. Indeed, unlike 135, 100 now houses large extended families with large numbers of youth, children, and adolescent single mothers and babies. The challenge of 100 was to create a sense of pride in one's building, to prevent the children from marking up the hallways with graffiti, and to prevent many of the adults or their visiting friends from being a nuisance during the late-night hours (loud radios, parties, and so forth).

Tenant organizing is an art. It requires planning, consistency, organizational skills, and sensitivity to individual family needs. Ruth Browne did the day-to-day "legwork" that made the tenant meetings a great success. The monthly two-hour tenant meetings were held in our church fellowship hall and always with both the building tenants *and* the housing committee members of our congregation (consisting of Vision Group members). The presence of so many concerned Memorial members contributed greatly to the notion in our neighborhood that our church really did care about the families and individuals who live there. Over fifty meetings were held with the tenants of 135. Numerous strategy sessions with the City of New York's Housing Preservation Department (HPD), the lawyers, and the tenant executive committee occurred before the dream of the 135 tenant-owned co-op became a reality.

Don Morlan, our consultant, also was with us through the agony and the ecstasy of this new birth. I was present for nearly every meeting in order to demonstrate my pastoral care for our neighbors next door. Imagine low-income people in Harlem buying their apartments from the City of New York for an incredible sum of $250 each! Memorial and ABC Metro New York helped make this happen.

In the previous chapter I spoke of gifting leaders. The tenant organization of 135 started the gifting process moving both within and beyond our church doors. In our church three members received their real estate licenses as well as special credentials to become 7A administrators (to manage city-owned housing). Several more members became tenant presidents of their own housing projects. They responded as they heard the message come home to them Sunday after Sunday that we must control our own neighborhoods, control our own destinies. All who sat through meeting after meeting learned a whole new lexicon of words and concepts related to housing work. But the gifting process went even further. Nine tenants attended special workshops on tenant management and cooperative ownership at a local college, and they became the grass-roots leaders in their apartment complex. Almost 100 percent attendance was realized as a local college provided technical "how-to" assistance in weatherstripping windows and doing one's own basic plumbing (changing a faucet washer, for example).

The tenants in 135 came alive. Of course, there were many stormy meetings leading to the cooperative battle. Most of the conflict was over individual apartment needs versus the care of the building as a whole. For instance, Ms. Carklin's (not her real name) apartment needed painting. The elevator needed to be fixed so senior citizens and the handicapped could readily get back and forth from their apartments. Monthly rent money that was collected had to be stretched to accommodate the most urgent needs first. Seeing people finally recognize that general good might take precedence over individual needs (although legitimate) reaffirmed my faith in human nature and specifically in urban persons.

The tenant organization of 100 initially had not been as successful as that of 135. In the case of 100, the building finally was owned and operated by the housing committee of the church, and hence, the residents often saw the church as a landlord rather than a catalyst for self-ownership. Because of the large size of the apartments and the extraordinary financial outlay that would be required to substantially renovate this building as a co-op, this would mean that most present low- and moderate-income families would have to relocate. The 135 building was not as run-down as 100, the apartments are smaller, and the building is more manageable with twenty-one units.

The 100 building was to be rehabilitated moderately by the City of New York, a local bank, and the church at a cost of $1.2 million. It took about four years to negotiate mortgage rates and repayment schedules; pay the back taxes; and maintain construction, architecture, and engineering costs in an inflationary economy. Housing committees must meet regularly to oversee the operation of so complex a process and be prepared to be refused a positive response to the best-laid plans by bureaucrats whose agenda may be different from that of the community.

Right at the point that we were ready to rehabilitate 100, we learned from the City of New York that the building had tax and emergency assistance arrears of nearly $400,000! All along we were told that we owed the city about $85,000. So the discovery by an anonymous computer of so large a shortfall was a real shock to our church and the ABC staff. We finally were able to work out a deal with the former commissioner of the Housing Preservation Department, and he allowed our church to "cancel" the debt and transfer the building (after a two-year series of HPD involvements to repair the roof, apartment floors, and so forth) into the hands of the tenants as a co-op. It is hoped that in the spring of 1988, the 100 St. Nicholas building will be owned by the tenants. The current president of the tenant's association is Marvin L. Hadley, minister of music of our church. The vice president, June Lum, also is a member of our church. Memorial is still present in 100, but now through the direct in-

volvement of church members who are themselves empowered to conduct their own affairs—indeed, to manage their
own building!

Success or Faithfulness?

By and large, housing work is a thankless task. Most
people are not prone to remember the bad times that triggered the church's involvement in seeking to stabilize their
homes in the first place. New tenants only know that if the
church is the landlord, it is responsible for busted pipes, the
broken boiler, and the dirty hallway.

Even the housing committee must be constantly replen-
ished with new people—for the rigorous meetings, the long
hours of work, the irate tenant pressures and the governmental bureaucratic entanglements that snarl the plans for
renovation produce large numbers of casualties. The congregation itself begins to wonder *Why all the bother about saving
those peoples' homes when most of them don't even attend our church?*
Besides, the break-even financial condition of a nonprofit
housing project makes it appear to be a waste of good human
effort. Why not do mission work somewhere else, where the
financial and spiritual returns might be more lucrative?

The challenge for Memorial and for all urban congregations is whether they will be willing to join hands with both
Christians and nonbelievers in saving communities like Harlem for the forgotten poor and the harassed lower-middle
class. Mission cannot be so easily equated with filling church
pews—or for that matter—church coffers.

Perhaps housing work represents the difficult cutting edge
for the urban church. Congregations like Memorial might be
even more effective if they worked in harmony with several
congregations in creating a joint housing strategy. Maybe so.
But that coming-alive church in Central Harlem experienced
the powerful outpouring of the Holy Spirit each time a
tenant began to communicate with his next-door neighbor
for the first time in twenty years, or when church members
invited me to speak to *their* tenant association about what

poor people can accomplish if they organize, or when a deacon (who was discipled as a new member) left a fabulous job as a merchant seaman to become the superintendent/security guard at both 100 and 135. Why? Because for him it represented a terrific ministry opportunity to be a role model for the buildings' youth and children.

Success seems so fleeting. The hard, dirty work of housing calls for faithfulness. Our Lord sends us into the hedges and highways. For the urban church the neighbor, the building, or the family right next door may be where the Lord is leading us. That, too, is the power of the transforming Spirit of God. (See The Study Guide, Session 5.)

The Transformation of the Spirit— Ministry Update

As of this writing (fall 1987), Memorial Baptist Church has reconstituted a Vision Group of some fifty-to-sixty people to ascertain what God might intend for our congregation on the verge of the twenty-first century. Based upon our congregational experiences in discipleship training and housing work through ownership, management, tenant advocacy, and self-ownership co-op development, we discovered that a major issue confronting the church and the community is the survival and development of the black family and the varieties of structures and arrangements organized by people for mutual support, cooperation, nurture, and growth of the black family. These days the nuclear family consisting of two parents with two children is more the exception than the rule in North America.[4] We began to see that there were many single-parent families in our community and within the church. Most of these households are headed by young-adult and teenage women who often needed emotional, spiritual, and economic support. In addition, these mothers are frequently in need of parenting skills, mentoring by older people, advocacy related to academic problems of their children, job training, nursery and/or child-care support, among other issues.

Our congregation, therefore, created an umbrella agency called Memorial Community Services, Inc. (MCS), to seek governmental and philanthropic grants to address the needs of single-parent families. We felt that a separate incorporated organization from the church would afford us greater flexibility in funding solicitations, especially given the fact that though the majority of the board of directors consisted of church members, community residents and professionals also participate in the organization's decision-making process.

Memorial Community Services, Inc. presently oversees the following program operations and ministries in our church.

1. *The Teen Pregnancy Prevention Program:* In conjunction with Abyssinian and Canaan Baptist churches, MCS has received a grant through the New York Urban League to provide teenage youth with training in character building, identity development, and personal communication skills. Parents also are involved in special "rap" sessions to better understand the developmental issues of teenagers, most particularly the biological and emotional changes that adolescents undergo as they become adults. This preventative program seeks to steer young people away from premature decisions regarding pregnancy and parenthood. Workshops on AIDS, human sexuality, Christian values, and family life frequently are offered through this ministry. This program has strengthened church and community youth. For example, not one teenager who had participated in this program to date has become pregnant. Parents are empowered to become more actively involved in their child's school and in developing a structured, disciplined home environment for their teenagers. More than 100 youth and parents are involved in this program, which is co-coordinated by a young deacon and a laywoman and

supervised by Rev. Mariah Ann Britton, Memorial's assistant pastor.

2. *Grandparents' Mentoring Program:* Through a grant from the Burden Foundation, MCS is operating a single-parent support network. This program is coordinated by a senior adult who is presently identifying older persons to serve as mentors to younger families. In actual fact, this program is mutually beneficial to both the young family and the mentor. The single parent and children have available to them an older person— a grandmother/grandfather type—who will be a support person to the young family by serving as a role model and being available to share information and problems. Many retired older adults live a distance from their offspring, hence, their involvement with a single-parent family gives them surrogate children and grandchildren. Through grandparent mentoring, the notion of the black church as an extended family is actualized. The wisdom of the elders and the enthusiasm of the young are mutually shared in the new family creation.

3. *The Memorial Home for Mothers and Babies:* Homelessness is a national tragedy.[5] One problem of homelessness is related to the fact that many newborn infants are abandoned in municipal hospitals, often due to their mothers' inability to find affordable housing. Our MCS board has recently submitted a proposal to the State of New York Department of Services for Families, Children and Youth, for the development of a Tier II Temporary Shelter for sixteen young adult mothers (age 18–25) and their sixteen babies. The proposed facilities will cost $1.5 million and provide temporary housing for young mothers and their infants for a maximum of one-and-a-half years. The goal of the project is to provide the young-adult parent with training to acquire a high school diploma, enroll in college, and/or become gainfully employed.

While the mother is preparing herself academically or through employment, the church will provide a child care service for the infants during the day. On evenings and weekends the mothers will establish their own cooperative nursery to take care of the children. The shelter will not only empower single parents by providing them with necessary academic and living skills (learning how to budget and save money, shop for well-balanced meals, write a job resume, and so forth), but it also will allow the family of mother and child to remain together while the former seeks permanent living quarters.

4. *Memorial Prison Outreach:* Our congregation also has "adopted" an area corrections facility in order to reach out to imprisoned young men. This program operates each fifth Sunday in the calendar year. A group of between five and twenty adult church members conduct worship services in the area facility and then engage in one-on-one counseling with those men who voluntarily decide to talk with us. These men usually are in the facility for not more than sixty days, at which time they will be released from prison. As they reenter society they need information about job and apartment prospects and ways of reconnecting with their families. Most important, they need to feel forgiven by a society that has preferred to expend $40,000 to $50,000 a year to imprison them, while reducing scholarship and grant support that could send them through four years of college for the same amount of money. MCS serves as an advocate for these young men, and though this program is in need of further strengthening, many friendships have already been established between the inmates and the members who serve in the prison outreach ministry. There also have been workshops for young people to inform them of their rights under law and to show them and their parents what they can do if arrested.

Though MCS is a newly created outreach arm of our congregation, its positive effects on the church and community are already being felt. Because of our collective efforts, we have signaled to local political leaders, social service organizations, and other congregations that we must strengthen and nurture our families and individuals. The local church can play an important broker role in developing intergenerational programs to realize these objectives.

Harlem Churches for Community Improvement, Inc. (HCCI)

It is becoming increasingly clear to me that no matter how successful or viable *any individual* church outreach program may be, there is yet a critical need for ecumenical church coalitions to be formed to empower congregations, families, and communities to bring about significant social and spiritual change. In December 1986 I was named president of Harlem Churches for Community Improvement, Inc. This ecumenical body of more than fifty congregations in the Harlem area contains large-membership congregations as well as storefront churches.[6] In a recent communique regarding HCCI, the following plan of action was outlined.

Harlem Churches for Community Improvement, Inc. (HCCI) was organized in December 1986. HCCI, an ecumenical organization of congregations in the Harlem area, is committed to the holistic revitalization of the community through the development of affordable housing and economic, social, and spiritual development. The constituency of HCCI consists of the full spectrum of community-based churches whose pastors and laity bring to this rehabilitation challenge a plethora of talents, skills, and expertise in housing development, construction, and management, in addition to social and economic revitalization capacities. At present HCCI has submitted a $100 million housing redevelopment proposal to the New York City Department of Housing Preservation and Development (HPD). Public and private funds are being solicited to complement the substantial contributions made by local congregations. Members of HCCI pay dues of $100 per congregation per year. In addition, member congregations have made an economic commitment to provide $3 per member for this redevelopment effort. These funds will be utilized for the comprehensive redevelopment of the area bounded by 145th and 155th Streets, between Bradhurst Avenue and Adam Clayton Powell Jr. Boulevard; the area surrounding Esplanade Gardens and the Harlem River Houses, and in close proximity to Yankee Stadium. This area is one of the most blighted and economically and socially depressed areas in the City of New York.

HCCI, working in conjunction with the Harlem Urban Development Corporation (HUDC), local social service and community groups, planners, developers, investors, and government officials, believes that this area can be successfully revitalized through this model of partnership in development.

This redevelopment plan has some important, unique features:

1. Seven hundred and seventy occupied apartments will be moderately rehabilitated, thus moving the residents toward management and ownership through the Tenants Interim Lease Program; 633 low-income rental units will be redeveloped in vacant buildings; 361 moderate-income cooperative units will be redeveloped; and 193 middle-income condominium units will be developed. The total number of units to be developed is 1,957.

2. The community will be shored up by bringing in mixed-income residents, thereby bringing about the overall economic revitalization of the Harlem community.

3. This plan would be parallel to the housing redevelopment initiative of HUDC and public initiatives taken by the city and private-sector initiatives. This affords us a unique opportunity to place housing stock on the tax rolls, encourage commercial development, and provide badly needed homes through ownership for a significant number of individuals and families.

4. This housing redevelopment plan is economically feasible and financially sound. It will produce economically affordable housing for the residents of the Harlem community. A smaller percentage of public subsidy is

involved due to the tax credit investments by private investors.

5. This project signals a partnership between the clergy and local constituency, political leadership, private sector, and government in working together to launch a comprehensive redevelopment scheme for a vast geographic area in a most depressed and deprived community.

Of course, the development of affordable housing is just one issue among others in urban communities like Harlem. Other nagging social issues like unemployment, drugs, crime, illiteracy, limited commercial development—not to mention the serious spiritual impoverishment that plagues places where hopelessness and despair are ever-present—are our concern as clergy and laity. Through this ecumenical church effort, we hope to generate necessary funds to rebuild Harlem.

The transforming power of the Spirit of God is at it again! This time my congregation and the community of Harlem, through churches and social, political, and business interests, are collaborating together to realize a second Harlem Renaissance.

Conclusion

A Work in Progress

I have an image in my mind. It is a vivid picture of the prophet Jeremiah down at the potter's shop (Jeremiah 18:1ff.). The spokesman for Yahweh observed that the skilled artisan was relentless in his commitment to perfect the unformed mass of wet earthen clay. The prophet could hear the loud sound of moistened formless clay being pounded on the potter's wheel. Then, after numberless attempts at making the clay conform to the vision in the potter's mind, the masterpiece was ready.

Jeremiah's potter's shop story might best describe our renewing church. God is at work remodeling, remaking, and recreating us that we may be faithful to our calling as the people of God, as Yahweh's work in progress.

As stated earlier, after several years of steady knocks and bruises in my first pastorate, I had the urge to move on to another church. Where the Lord leads me in the future is not yet clearly known. I express my gratitude to the kind Spirit of God and the care of the people of my parish to resist the temptation to flee from a church in the process of renewal, growth, and development *before* I really had become a pastor and leader of Memorial and its surrounding community in a full, wholesome, and effective sense.

The people of Memorial are discovering this living truth

that the Spirit of God *produces tension.* Tension proved positive for us, for it moved many dormant people to activity. The Spirit even drove the church congregation beyond its four safe walls into the crisis-laden arena of a community experiencing the birth pangs of transformation.

The Spirit of God transforms near-dead institutions (like Memorial). It invigorates and revitalizes inactive, "frozen," or angry believers as well. It heals wounds and reconciles former church enemies to become colleagues in a common ministry and mission cause. The Spirit of God gifts humble persons to become liberators and builders of new communities. This is revolution!! This is the transformation of the Spirit of God! I pray that every dying church in America might experience the refreshing and powerful winds of God's transforming Spirit. And more than once.

Appendix

The Study Guide

Session 1: "Leadership Development for the Kingdom"

Session 2: "Stewardship of Our Time"

Session 3: "Stewardship of Our Talents"

Session 4: "The Envisioning Process"*

Session 5: "Stewardship of Relationships—The Neighbor"

The following session plans can be reshaped to meet your specific group's/congregation's needs. Make certain that all the necessary materials, such as newsprint, markers, tape, Bibles, paper, pens, and pencils, are available.

Session 1: "Leadership Development for the Kingdom"

Jesus began to preach, saying, "Repent, for the kingdom of heaven is at hand" (Matthew 4:17).

Repent!

To "repent" means to make an about-face, to turn to God, to begin anew, to seek forgiveness. Every believer is called upon to repent,

*Session 4 can be more than one session.

but the leader in the Christian community is especially in need of repentance and forgiveness. To lead God's people one first must be led by God. One's motives, attitudes, opinions, decisions, and actions must be brought into alignment with God's will. Our goal is to "let Thy will be done, On earth as it is in heaven" (Matthew 6:10).

Jesus' message of repentance was the repetition of the same theme by John the Baptizer. But as John put it, "I baptize you with water for repentance, but he who is coming after me is mightier than I . . . he will baptize you with the Holy Spirit and with fire" (Matthew 3:11). The "he" John was referring to is Jesus, and the repentance Jesus demands is total. It must encompass the heart and head, the will and wish, the mind and body. Everything about us is changed. Nicodemus learned this in the late-night sermon when Jesus said, "You must be born again!" (paraphrase of John 3:3).

There can be no born-again churches until there are born-again believers. Both the pulpit and the pew need the refreshing and invigorating power of the Holy Spirit. There can be no transformed churches until there are changed believers—and especially renewed leaders. Renewal begins in earnestly inviting the Lord of life to take charge of us, to lead us, to strengthen us, to empower us, to engage us, to forgive us.

Make Disciples

"Go therefore and make disciples of all nations . . ." (Matthew 28:19). The kingdom demands immediate action of the transformed believer! "Go" and "make" are demands, commands, imperatives. Leadership in the church often seeks to keep the church building operating. Fund-raising drives, building funds, special projects, appeals, pledges, and financial goals are attempts to keep the church building and programs afloat. However much we give our time, talent, and finances to these goals, may we never forget "that our purpose for being the church is to make disciples. Budgets, machines, new carpets, remade windows, special lighting, buses, new hymnbooks; whatever material goals we seek to reach, our ultimate goal is to win men and women and boys and girls for service to the kingdom. *The goal of the church is to make disciples, to build the new community of faith, love, and reconciliation.*

Grace—Cheap or Costly?

The contemporary church confesses its faith in Jesus. It pays him impressive lip service. But when one becomes a disciple, one acts in obedience to the will of God. Jesus calls. We follow. Jesus called Levi; he left his receipts and followed (Mark 2:14). Jesus called Peter, James, and John; they left their boats and followed (Matthew 4:18–22). Jesus calls us. How do we respond? Dietrich Bonhoeffer, the German pastor, teacher, and resistance leader against Adolf Hitler, made a clear distinction between "cheap" and "costly" grace.

Cheap grace is a religion we can enjoy because it makes no demands on us. It comes cheaply. "Cheap grace is the preaching of forgiveness without requiring repentance; baptism without church discipline; communion without confession. . . . Cheap grace is grace without discipleship, grace without the Cross, grace without Jesus Christ, living and incarnate."[1]

Costly grace was exemplified by Jesus. We have been bought through Christ's death. The grace of Christ is costly. It "compels a man [or woman] to submit to the yoke of Christ," says Bonhoeffer, "and follow Him; it is grace because Jesus says: 'My yoke is easy and my burden is light.' "[2] Ours is a costly grace; an expensive commitment to Christ. It shows in the quality of our time, talent, and resources given for the cause of God's kingdom. We give God our very best through service!

Leadership for the kingdom does not begin with understanding the requirements for the office we hold. It does not begin with listing the tasks we are to perform. It begins with recognizing our calling as sons and daughters of God who respond in faith to the life-transforming power of the Holy Spirit. When the Holy

Spirit comes into the lives of men and women, then gifts are identified to carry out the specific work of kingdom-building. In Ephesians 4:11–12 Apostle Paul said, "It was he who 'gave gifts to mankind'; he appointed some to be apostles, others to be prophets, others to be evangelists, others to be pastors and teachers. He did this to prepare all God's people for the work of Christian service, in order to build up the body of Christ" (TEV).

Leadership is a stewardship within the church of Jesus Christ. Each member has a *ministry* and a *mission.* God calls each of us to carry out the divine will. The way the Holy Spirit uses us and empowers us helps us to identify our gifts/talents and creatively use our time. All positions within the living body of Christ have a purpose and are therefore necessary parts of the whole. In our free church tradition, we recognize Jesus the Christ as the head of the Church. All decisions, actions, and practices for our life and ministry begin and end with him. We recognize him as Savior and Lord of our lives and Shepherd of the flock.

The membership: All persons who are born-again, baptized believers and who seek to bear and share the kingdom of God are given divine authority to govern the church. At the time of their baptism, these persons have publicly acknowledged both their ordination (set apart for special work) and their coronation (crowning as children of God). Recognizing this, the members understand that they have a special and important ministry to carry out.

The pastor: The pastor is called of God to be the "undershepherd" of the flock. The church is not his or her possession. The pastor is the spiritual overseer of God's church. He or she is the head—the seer, the visionary, the motivator. She or he trains, enlists, and supports the membership. His or her job is to equip the saints and help them carry out their tasks. *The job of the pastor is to develop leaders for the work of the kingdom.*

The diaconate: Though some congregations view only men as deacons (and call women deaconesses), the work of the diaconate is essentially the same, regardless of gender (1 Timothy 3:8–13).

There are many persons in our churches who also serve as leaders: auxiliary and club presidents, associate ministers, youth coordinators, missionary presidents, choir directors, Christian education leaders, church school teachers, and so forth. In the Christian context, "a leader is a person who uses her or his gifts to enable others in ministry."[3] Let's take this definition apart.

The stewardship of leadership is "to enable others." To enable, according to Ephesians 4, is to "prepare all God's people." Rev. Jones reminds us that "the dictionary defines 'enable' as 'to give power, strength, or competency.' Our job as Christian leaders is to enable others to carry out their ministries, to use their special gifts." Again, Jones says, "But, in truth, the power, strength, and competency that is needed within is a gift of God."[4] As leaders, we can encourage, support, identify, and develop another person's gifts and "calling." We cannot produce it or make it happen.

The stewardship of leadership is to serve others. To serve is to lead (John 13:2–17; Matthew 23:11). Only as we "help persons become what God intended them to be can the leader fulfill his/her role as an enabler."[5] Jesus taught and lived the life of the servant, selflessly giving of himself that others might discover the kingdom of God both in and around them.

Leadership seeks to develop a servant church: Leadership in the Christian context enables persons to serve the world. "God so loved the world . . ." (John 3:16). So ought we. There's a hurt, battered, unloving, cruel world waiting for us. But it also is a world of surprises, wonderment, joy, love, hope, and concern. Whether we join the PTA or local political club, serve on a jury, volunteer at a service center, teach a child to improve reading skills, or become a pen pal to a brother or sister who is incarcerated, we are called out of the comfort of the church into the unpredictable arena where the voice of God's love and human sensitivity is needed now more than ever before. It's expensive grace. But as Jesus reminds us,

"Then I, the King, shall say to those at my right, 'Come, blessed of my Father, into the Kingdom prepared for you from the founding of the world. For I was hungry and you fed me; I was thirsty and you gave me water; I was a stranger and you invited me into your homes; naked and you clothed me; sick and in prison, and you visited me' " (Matthew 25: 34–36, *The Living Bible*).

The world is seeking repentant, born-again, called, sent-out leaders who are willing to serve, willing to enable, willing to take risks for the kingdom!

Reflection / Action

Prayerfully answer the following. Don't rush!

1. What does it mean to repent? Besides Jesus, who else in the Gospels used this word as a condition for being baptized?
2. When the term "born-again" is used, what does this mean to you? Who was Nicodemus? What type of leader was he? Have you been "born-again?"
3. Earlier it was stated that "the goal of the church is to make disciples." What does this mean? Explain in your own words.
4. According to Dietrich Bonhoeffer, what's the difference between cheap and costly grace?
5. Read Ephesians 4. What does this chapter, written by Apostle Paul, tell us about the role, function, and ministry of the church and Christian?
6. Who is called to be a leader in the church?
7. Are *you* a leader?
8. What is the role of Jesus the Christ, the pastor, the diaconate, and other club/auxiliary leaders in the leadership of the church? List and be specific.
9. What role does the membership play in the Free Church tradition?
10. Give a definition of leadership.
11. What is enablement?
12. What does it mean to serve others? Be specific.

13. What is the role of leadership within the church? Outside the church?
14. Do you have any questions about the stewardship of leadership?

Session 2: "Stewardship of Our Time"

Discuss briefly how *one* gift of each participant can be used in our church.

Where Did the Time Go?

Believe it or not, we never can become good stewards until we learn to manage our time. Time is limited. The rapid movement of each person from birth to death suggests that we have all too little time. There are twenty-four hours in a day, sixty minutes in an hour, and sixty seconds in a minute. Have you often asked "where did the time go?" One thing is certain: Time is irretrievable. We can't get it back. Neither can we turn the clock back. We shouldn't worry about time—we should be concerned about ourselves. After all, the time in our lives didn't go anywhere. It was our use or misuse of it that made the difference.

This session deals with the stewardship of time. It affirms the words of Scripture, "Make the best possible use of your time" (Colossians 4:5, Phillips). Another way to put this is make the best possible use of your life and the time question effectively will be handled.

- Read Matthew 25:1–13
- Select two persons to serve as leaders, one as a "wise" maiden, and another as a "foolish" maiden.
- Have group divide into two sections, one led by leader #1, the other led by leader #2.
- Ask both groups why some maidens were wise and others foolish.
- Who is involved in this story? Can it be referred to as a parable?
- Who is telling this story?

- What might be some of the purposes for which the story was told?
- Who might the "bridegroom" in the story be?
- What does the wedding feast in the story suggest?
- How do you relate to the story?

Highlights: The setting is Jerusalem. Jesus and his band of followers have just left the temple. Chapters 24 and 25 of Matthew's Gospel weave together several of Jesus' parables and statements. The central thread that holds these stories together is the idea that the end is coming quickly. The end is sometimes referred to as the *parousia:* the return of Jesus and the end of history and time as we presently know and understand it. But the concern of the parables is not to predict the end (24:36), nor to manipulate present circumstances to rush the end (24:23–28), but rather to wait and be prepared for the return of Christ.

The parable of the ten maidens (or ten virgins) was told by Jesus. This is one of the few cases when Jesus directly refers to his parable characters as wise or foolish. It appears that the ten maidens differed in their understanding. All of them went out to meet the bridegroom. However, the groom was delayed. All the maidens went to sleep. Eventually, the groom appeared. At his announcement, the foolish maidens realized that they were nearly out of oil. Having no easy solution to their problem, they went late at night in search of an oil merchant. By the time they returned, the groom had joined the wise maidens and the festivities had begun. The late maidens discovered that they had been excluded from the wedding celebration.

The ten maidens had an opportunity to get enough oil to prepare for the coming of the bridegroom, but only five took the time to do so. This was a wise decision. The other five maidens did not take the time to prepare, and hence were panic-stricken when the bridegroom returned. They made a foolish decision. They superficially supposed that if they were short of oil their friends would supply them, or they could easily locate an oil merchant. Neither of these options proved successful. They refused to take their lives seriously. They refused to plan their time. They thought they could predict the attitude of the bridegroom. They assumed that their tardiness would be excused. They were wrong. Their tragedy was that they believed they would be taken care of no matter what they did.

We know very little about first-century Jewish wedding customs. However, what might be the role of the maidens in this story? Who does the bridegroom symbolize? What is the marriage feast representative of for the believer? What lessons for our lives do we get from this story?

Note: The maidens could not adequately predict when the bridegroom would come; nor could they make him come. They could only wait. But waiting is not inactivity. It is not doing nothing. In the Scriptures, waiting is active preparation and planning for the return of Christ. All the maidens went to sleep. That was fine. We need the refreshment of sleep and relaxation. But the wise maidens made certain that they had a sufficient supply of oil to light their lamps before they went to sleep.

Time planning is a Christian responsibility. As the wise maidens knew, their time really was not their own. They were employed by the bridegroom. Hence, their time was really his time. Our time is really God's time. The management and planning of our time is a prayerful and powerful decision on our part. In planning we ask our Creator What is your will for my life? What do you want me to do? The doing of God's will in our lives is a time-management decision. How do you spend your time?

1. Probe the depths of your soul. Search. Seek. What is God saying to you about your life? What is God getting you to understand about the divine will for you? Write down your comments.

2. In no particular order, list all the things you do on a daily basis (for example, change the baby's diapers, cook dinner, drive the car, go to work; go to school, attend the Golden Age Club, and so forth).

Study/Reflection/Action

1. Refer back to 1. Is this statement exact or can you make it more specific?
2. Refer back to 2. Review your laundry list of daily activities. Are there other activities you can add to this list? Don't forget sleeping, eating, and so forth. As you refer to 2, place the things you do in the categories below:
   early morning (before 9:00 A.M.)
   morning (9:00 A.M.–12:00 noon)
   afternoon (12:00 noon–6:00 P.M.)
   evening (6:00 P.M.–midnight)
   late night (after midnight)
3. Put checkmarks next to those activities that you just listed that you must perform in order to survive (for example, eat, sleep, and so forth).
4. Put an X next to those activities that relate to your responsibilities as a member of a family or part of a household.
5. Put a circle around those activities that reflect what you believe is God's will for your life.

If your schedule changes daily, what are the other activities that you engage in that are not on the list?

1. What are the missing pieces in your daily life?
2. How much time do you spend with your family, friends, church members, yourself, and God?
3. What are the activities related to your spiritual development and nurture that you neglected? (For example, prayer, service to others, attending worship, and so forth).

4. Add information based on 1, 2, and 3 to your time list.
5. Keep this list with you during the week. Add/subtract as your days unfold. Did you follow this schedule? If not, how did you change it? Were you a little more conscious about how you spent your time? How did you waste time?

Christians often have assumed that if they did not work for or in a religious organization professionally, they were not doing God's will. However, place of employment is not the only determinant of our "call" by God. We may work in various jobs, be in school, or may be retired. Yet, by finding that avocation—that special activity, job, or commitment—we can still make our life count for God. This is true even if our regular job is boring or unfulfilling. Jesus was a carpenter, but he found time to preach, teach, and heal. Paul was a tentmaker, but he creatively used his time to build churches, write important church letters, and organize mission projects. Our jobs should not be an excuse for *not* doing God's will. Beyond your *job,* what can/are you doing with your time for God's kingdom?

In your job, school, or retirement, what can or are you doing with your time for God's kingdom?

"Working for God makes even our spare time count. In helpfulness to others, every [person] can find on [one's] own doorstep adventures for the soul—our surest source of peace and lifelong satisfaction. This career of the Spirit I call "Your second job!" There is no pay except the privilege of doing it. Here all your reserve powers can be put to work, for what the world lacks most today are [people] who occupy themselves with the needs of other [people]."[6]

Session 3: "Stewardship of Our Talents"

Invite five people to act out Matthew 25:14–30:

1. the narrator
2. the master

3. the five-talent servant
4. the two-talent servant
5. the one-talent servant

Though the story is a parable of Jesus, have these five people add their own words or ideas to make the story come alive. As these five people are preparing their script, divide the remaining group into three sections:

1. The "Hearers"—what do they hear in the conversation of the story?
2. The "Seers"—what do they see (the body language, for example) of each person in the story?
3. The "Feelers"—what emotions are expressed by each person in the story?

Highlights for Discussion: Jesus, Master Storyteller

Jesus was a master storyteller. His ministry was marked by an interesting storytelling style, often referred to as "parables." The stories that Jesus wove before his hearers were illustrations from everyday life. But they always pointed beyond the ordinary circumstances of daily existence. Though he rarely directly used God's name or imposed a moral on his parable, Jesus used this device to reach his hearers right where they were. It was a fresh approach. He did not use jargon or difficult religious concepts, dogma, or creeds. He simply told a story from life and wrapped it in a heavenly package.

As you heard, saw, and felt the parable of the talents, what type of person did the master seem to be? Does the master's personality change during the story? If so, how?

What do you notice about the people with the five talents and the two talents? What types of personalities might you suspect they had? What about the one-talent man? Did he do anything wrong by hiding his talent?

The story of the talents may have been told by Jesus to criticize the Hebrew people for refusing "to be good stewards of their covenant heritage," as Dan Otto Via, Jr.[7] describes it. By rejecting outsiders and clinging to their law and traditions, the Jews may have lost, in Jesus' thinking, their authentic heritage as God's Chosen People.

In the story, all three people are given talents according to their ability. As the Revised Standard Version defines it, a talent was more than fifteen years' wages of a laborer.

The master entrusted the talents to them without verbal instructions. It seems clear that he trusted them to understand that their responsibility was to help their investments grow.

The two-talent and five-talent men immediately went to the marketplace and engaged in barter, invested what they had, and took the risks with the talents. The story sees life as risky as a marketplace experience, wherein we sometimes win and sometimes lose.

What happened to the investments of the two-talent and five-talent men? What do you think the master might have said to these men if they had lost his investments?

When the Master returned he asked all three men to give an account of their stewardship. The one-talent man (verse 18) had hidden his talent in the ground, so he simply returned what he had. He said that he refused to take the risk because he was afraid and assumed the owner would be angry with him if he lost the investment. Dan Otto Via, Jr. describes the one-talent man:

> He was afraid. Therefore, he acted to preserve his safety. Or to be more precise, he acted as little as possible. He sought to avoid the risk of trading in the market and expected to stay at least minimally in his master's good graces by preserving exactly what had been entrusted to him. He hoped for a safe bargain.[8]

Via sees interesting parables to our own lives in the one-talent man's example.

> In the fear of the one-talent man, we see the anxiety of one who will not step into the unknown. He will not risk trying to fulfill his own possibilities, therefore, his existence is circumscribed in the narrowest kind of way.[9]

The one-talent man started as a free man, but he refused to be responsible.

The movement of the man is from refusal to take a risk (verse 18), through guilt (verse 23), to projection—putting the blame on someone else (verse 24), to the loss of opportunity for responsible living (verses 26–28).

Study/Reflection

- What does the "well done" statement of the master mean to you?
- Describe the curse of the one-talent man.
- What does this parable tell us about the Christian's concepts of life, responsibility, and courage?
- What are your "talents?"
- Do we always utilize our talents or are they frequently buried or hidden?
- What do we fear by employing them?

Action!

Gifts, talents, skills, strong points, or abilities are *presents* from a gracious God.

Gifts List: During the week, think about as many of your gifts/talents as you can. Don't just think about gifts that might be directly used in church (teaching Sunday school, for example). Other gifts you possess should be explored. Use as much space as you need, and list each gift in section 1 that follows.

Each person possesses many gifts. Often these remain unrecognized or underutilized. Brainstorm! List your gifts freely as they come to your mind.

A tentmaker preacher: Apostle Paul was a tentmaker by profession. He described his life this way:

> To the present hour we hunger and thirst, we are ill-clad and buffeted and homeless, and we labor, working with our own hands. When reviled, we bless; when persecuted, we endure . . . (1 Corinthians 4:11–12).

Yet Paul also was God's chief exponent of the liberating gospel of Jesus Christ to both Jews and Gentiles. Paul was a tentmaker by vocation. Paul also had an avocation—and ultimate purpose—as a missionary/preacher/teacher/church builder/theologian.

A cobbler was asked, "what's your business?" "My business," he quickly responded, "is to extend the kingdom of God. I only cobble shoes to pay the expenses."[10]

1. My gifts (list them)
2. My skills (name where you use them)

Session 4: "The Envisioning Process"

This process is designed to help persons use the pictorial as well as the verbal and word portions of their minds. Planning can be a pleasant, fun-filled event if we will allow ourselves to enter into some new behaviors. Images and pictures usually do not come to our minds when we think about the present realities of our churches or our associations. We usually use words and ideas to analyze what we see happening around us.

However, we invite you to draw some images that tell the story of how you see things in the present and how you would like to see things in the future. You are going to be asked to develop and talk about two pictures: an *Is* picture (your perception of how things are now), and a *Vision* picture that shows your perception of how you would like to see things. The explanation for doing this follows.

1. This process goes on forever. In one sense, you are beginning a process that will have an effect on the life of your church and state organization for some time to come. The time needed for going through this process is approximately four hours (with eight people). The time can be broken into more than one session. For instance, two Wednesday evenings could be used, or a day-long or weekend retreat could be used. If

your group is larger than eight people, you should add an additional half hour to the time for each additional person or arrange to break down into groups of eight that will report their findings to the whole group.

2. You will need large sheets of newsprint, crayons or markers, and masking tape.

3. You now are ready to begin. Choose a group facilitator or leader who will move the process along and keep you on time. You will begin by drawing your *Is* picture. Make this picture a clear statement of how you see the organization or group upon which you are focusing. Think in pictures or symbols that you can share with the entire group. Try not to use words.

Develop and Share Individual Is *Pictures.*

1. Draw images to indicate how you see your church.
2. Place yourself in the picture.
3. Each person shares his or her *Is* picture with the entire group.
4. Group members ask clarification questions.
5. Leader lists common images or ideas that are included on more than one picture.
6. Review the *Is* pictures from the common list (collective listing by all members in the group).

Develop Individual and Group Vision *Pictures.*

1. Give explanation of the *Vision* picture. There are no restraints; forget issues such as budget, personnel, time, and so forth. Develop a picture that is totally as you wish or dream things could be. Let your imagination run wild. Place yourself in your *Vision* picture.
2. Put up individual pictures with tape.
3. Each person individually shares their *Vision* picture with the entire group.
4. Group leader lists common *Vision* images or ideas. (For example, one of the strong *Vision* ideas had to do with

shaping some new mission strategies for the congregation.)

5. The leader chooses one person to begin developing a common *Vision* picture. Try to choose the person who seems most comfortable with drawing images.

A. Using the list of the common *Vision* images and ideas, begin drawing a *Vision* picture that includes as many of the group's *Vision* images and ideas as possible.

B. Constantly check with the group as you draw the common *Vision* picture, until the group agrees that the picture is representative of the group's vision and includes the essential vision ideas of all of the individual *Vision* pictures.

List the Forces Either Blocking or Enabling Realization of the Vision Picture.

1. On two separate sheets of newsprint, list the forces (factors/issues/realities) enabling or helping to bring the *Vision* picture into reality.

2. On a separate sheet of newsprint, list the forces blocking or inhibiting the movement to bringing the *Vision* picture into reality.

3. Spend adequate time on 1 and 2 so that a fairly complete list of enabling and blocking forces is listed.

4. Now ask the group to choose the three major blocking forces working against the realization of the vision. Assign each person three votes and ask them to cast the votes for the three listed blocking forces that they consider, in their judgment, to be the greatest blocks to the realization of the vision. Cast your votes by actually putting marks beside the blocking force that is the person's choice. Add the votes cast and identify the three blocking forces with the greatest number of votes.

Create "How-to" Problem Statements.

1. Take each one of the top three blocking forces chosen and put "How to" in front of each. (For example, "negative attitude displayed by the board of deacons" could become a how-to problem statement by making it "How to change the board of deacons' negative attitude into a positive response.")
2. A simple problem-solving process using the problem statements chosen follows.

   A. Write the problem statement on a sheet of newsprint.
   B. Do some further analysis on the problem statement. List some of the historical facts that make this a problem. Be sure everyone understands why the statement is a problem to be solved.
   C. Pick one person in the group to be the "problem poser." This should be a person who feels strongly that this is a problem.
   D. Explain to the problem poser that his or her job is to listen to suggested solutions to this problem given by the group. If the solution offered seems workable, accept it and begin making a list of possible solutions. If the problem poser does not like the suggestions given by the group members, he or she should tell two things he or she likes about the possible solution before sharing dislikes.
   E. The group then should do some wishing about the problem statement. (For example, I wish the board of deacons would hold some open forums.) The wishes are important triggers for the generation of possible solutions. Wishes should be very free, open, unrealistic statements. The group leader will write down everyone's wishes. The more wishing the group can do, the more creative the possible solutions that will be given.

F. Outline of the problem-solving process:

1) turn blocking force into a "how-to" problem statement
2) pick a person who is not the group enabler or leader to be a problem poser
3) do a brief analysis of why this is a problem
4) begin having the group do some wishes
5) write on newsprint all of the stated wishes
6) begin suggesting possible solutions to the problem poser
7) make a list of the possible solutions acceptable.

Turn Possible Solutions into Objectives

1. The possible solutions generated by the group during the problem-solving session are basic objectives for the group or the organization. (For example, design a series of congregational meetings in which the board of deacons will dialogue with the congregation about present and future mission strategies.)
2. These objectives then become the action plan for the congregation. The group may want to go as far as assigning these objectives to boards or committees in the church, with time-lines and points of evaluation.

This same process can be used to generate new objectives when the original objectives have been accomplished. Our hope is that the planning group might continue to meet and evaluate the progress being made as well as develop new objectives.

Session 5: "Stewardship of Relationships—The Neighbor"

Read Luke 10:25–29. "Who is my neighbor?" was the question put to Jesus by a lawyer. Jesus' response was in the form of a story—the parable of the good Samaritan.

Read the story once. Then reread it. Select people to pantomime the parts of narrator, Samaritan, Levite, priest, muggers, the half-dead man, and the innkeeper.

Study lessons on the Jericho Road. It seems that Jesus would use the illustration of a Samaritan to explain the meaning of neighborliness. The Jews and Samaritans had had an adverse relationship for centuries. Matthew's Gospel is less kind to Samaritans; but Luke sees Jesus as a champion of the Gentiles. The lawyer asked Jesus "Who is my neighbor?", but Jesus responded with an example of what it means to be neighborly. In other words the usual focus would be on the person receiving the concern from others. Instead, Jesus put emphasis on the example of one who demonstrated "love in action." The one demonstrating love was a hated Samaritan.

A certain man, presumably a Jew, was traveling down the Jericho Road. He was mugged, robbed, stripped, beaten, and left half-dead. A *priest* saw the man but passed on the other side. Priests were the spiritual leaders of Israel. They were men who represented care and concern for the laws and for the people. Some commentators have suggested that perhaps the priest was late for synagogue worship, so he could not linger to help. A *Levite,* one who maintained the oil in the temple to see that the light never went out, also refused to aid the mugged brother. So both a clergyperson and a layperson had not time or inclination to help.

To be sure, it was dangerous business trying to help someone on the Jericho Road. It once was called "The Bloody Pass." One could wait for someone with good will to come along and then rob the unsuspecting helper. Maybe the priest and Levite felt that this was a possible setup. No matter what the reason, the priest's and Levite's failure to assist a brother suggests that to be a neighbor is not a cultural or racial question. It's a question of concern that goes well beyond *who* the person in need might be. The Samaritan might have had similar questions about his own safety, but he saw a man bleeding and dying. Jesus said, "He had com-

136

passion" (Luke 10:33). Dr. Martin Luther King, Jr., said this about the Samaritan:

> The Samaritan had the capacity for a *universal altruism*. He had a piercing insight into that which is beyond the eternal accidents of race, religion and nationality. One of the great tragedies of man's long trek along the highway of history has been the limiting of neighborly concern to tribe, race, class or nation. We see men as Jews or Gentiles, Catholics or Protestants, Chinese or American, Negroes or Whites. We fail to think of them as fellow human beings made from the same basic stuff as we, molded in the same divine image. The priest and the Levite saw only a bleeding body, not a human being like themselves. But the good Samaritan will always remind us to remove the cataracts of provincialism from our spiritual eyes and see men as men.[11]

To be sure, the good Samaritan possessed both " a universal altruism," and a "dangerous altruism," as Dr. King suggested. "The ultimate measure of a man is not where he stands in moments of comfort and convenience, but where he stands at times of challenge and controversy. The true neighbor will risk his position, his prestige, and even his life for the welfare of others."[12]

The Samaritan did not simply help the mugged man on the road. He also provided continued care and assistance. His concern was not superficial, neither was he seeking recognition, a plaque, or a pat on the back. We never come to know who the assisted individual was. We never even get a clue that the muggee even thanked the Samaritan for his unusual generosity and concern. Helping often is a thankless business. In the crowded ways of life, the assisted may never directly thank us for our care, our service, our outreach.

Think of a time when you came to the aid of someone in need. Recall the events. Was there the possibility of danger? Was it a question of association "with the wrong people"? How did you feel? What did you do to help? What results did you achieve? What did you do wrong?

One wonders how the Samaritan felt after he rendered assistance. Helping can provide a tremendous boost to our lives. It's dangerous, difficult, and often dreary, but it also is fulfilling and fundamental to our human search for meaning and purpose.

Who are the strangers who ride the subways and buses, who walk the streets, who live next door? What do they look like? What languages do they speak? What does helping the stranger mean in our city in our time? Who are the "mugged," the "stripped," or the "beaten" in our communities? How can being a good neighbor make sense given their needs and problems?

As you think about the individual strangers in our midst, what are the social and/or political issues that equally affect their lives? For example, the reason the man was mugged on the Jericho Road was because not enough had been done to secure the safety of those who were dependent on this route. Is the Christian's responsibility simply to focus on bleeding and hurt individuals, or also to address ourselves to the social and political forces that give rise to these conditions? Give an example.

Study/Reflection

During the week, read Luke 10:25–29.

1. Are there any other ideas you get from the story not previously mentioned?
2. How might we recast this parable to fit our present culture?
3. Does Jesus' idea of neighborliness seem naive in our times?
4. What type of neighbor are you?
5. What type of neighborliness do you find in your church?
6. How are strangers viewed by you and your fellow Christian brothers and sisters of this church?

Action!

A "stranger" remains one until we get to understand her or him and her or his culture; traditions; language; lifestyle; and ways of understanding the world, God, and other people.

Christians are a minority in the world today. We cannot so easily assume that the people of the world are all becoming like us as Christian people.

During this week think about our neighbors next door to our church. Visit places where your neighbor shops, socializes, or worships. Can you get to know one person who might become your friend or "significant other" who can better introduce you to his or her family? What might you share from your background? (If you feel uncomfortable or turned off by this exercise, try to locate your feelings. Why are you feeling this way?)

Write down your feelings about becoming involved with one selected next-door neighbor. Pray for guidance. How do you break the ice to make an acquaintance? How do you open up dialogue for sharing? What were your experiences as you tried to share?

Notes

Foreword

[1]Preston Robert Washington, *From the Pew to the Pavement* (Morristown, N.J.: Aaron Press, 1986).

[2]Henri Nouwen, *Creative Ministry* (New York: Doubleday and Company, 1971), pp. 61–62.

Preface

[1]I use the terms "transformation," "renewal," "growth," and "development" as a continuum. In the instance of Memorial, the renewal of the church—its revival and revitalization—preceded great growth, but it laid the foundation for its realization. A group of members became the leaven for the future growth of the congregation. Development means the perfecting or reshaping of programs, attitudes, and ministries to enhance further growth in the church and the transformation of the community. It is posited here that only through God's transforming Spirit can true renewal take place in the local church.

[2]*Webster's Seventh New Collegiate Dictionary* (Springfield, Mass.: Merriam-Webster Company, 1967), p. 726.

[3]Duncan McIntosh and Richard Rusbuldt, *Planning Growth in Your Church* (Valley Forge: Judson Press, 1983).

[4]Gene E. Bartlett, *The Audacity of Preaching* (New York: Harper and Row, Publishers Inc., 1962), p. 83.

Introduction

[1]Peter J. Paris, *The Social Teaching of the Black Churches* (Philadelphia: Fortress Press, 1985), p. 10. See also Vincent Harding, *The Other American Revolution* (Los Angeles: University of California Center for Afro-American Studies, 1980), pp. 14–15.

[2]E. Franklin Frazier, *The Negro Church in America* (New York: Schocken Books, 1963), p. 116.

[3]*Ibid.*, pp. 115–116.

[4]C. Peter Wagner, *Your Church Can Grow: Seven Vital Signs of a Healthy Church* (Ventura, Calif.: Regal Books, 1984), pp. 110–116. Wagner notes that the so-called "homogeneous unit" is most effective when people do not have to cross social or cultural barriers. They see one another as "our kind of people." Wagner contends this is not a racist maneuver; but within the context of white middle-class America and the "segregated hour" (Sunday 11 A.M.), one wonders if his claim is tenable, let alone believable.

[5]Delos Miles, *Church Growth—A Mighty River* (Nashville: Broadman Press, 1981), pp. 141–142. Miles critiques Robert Schuller's Garden Grove Community Church for seeing itself as a "non-prophet's church." He notes that the failure of the church-growth movement to take seriously the prophetic tension of the Old Testament, or even the strand of prophecy in the New Testament, is ludicrous and not true to the biblical witness.

[6]Ralph H. Elliott, *Church Growth That Counts* (Valley Forge: Judson Press, 1982), especially Chapter 3.

[7]Leonardo Boff, *Ecclesiogenesis: The Base Communities Reinvent the Church* (Maryknoll, N.Y.: Orbis Books, 1986).

Chapter 1

[1]Adam Clayton Powell, Sr., *Upon This Rock* (New York: Theo. Gaus' Sons, Inc., 1949), p. 126. Rev. W. Willard Monroe is cited by Powell as having served Abyssinian for three years beginning in 1926.

Chapter 2

[1]Harold A. Carter, *The Prayer Tradition of Black People* (Valley Forge: Judson Press, 1976), p. 55. This fine analysis of black prayer life, both its theological and social influences, is a good way to understand why Afro-American Christians traditionally have put great emphasis on the power of prayer and the verbal eloquence that accompanies it.

[2]A good introduction to prayer, especially for teenagers, is Bennie E. Goodwin, *Pray Right! Live Right! Reflections on the Lord's Prayer* (Downer's Grove, Ill.: Inter-Varsity Press, 1979).

[3]Rudolph E. Grantham, *Lay Shepherding* (Valley Forge: Judson Press, 1980).

Chapter 3

[1]Walter Wink, *The Bible in Human Transformation: Toward a New Paradigm for Biblical Study* (Philadelphia: Fortress Press, 1973).

[2]*Answering God's Call,* ABC Metro Church Development, December 1979, ABC Metro New York.

[3]Nathan W. Turner, *Effective Leadership in Small Groups* (Valley Forge: Judson Press, 1977). See especially Chapter 4, "Creative Use of Conflict."

Chapter 4

[1]Walter A. Henrichsen, *Disciples Are Made—Not Born* (Wheaton, Ill.: Victor Books, 1978). Another excellent resource for new member orientation classes is Alan R. Knight and Gordon H. Schroeder, *The New Life: Six Studies on the New Life in Christ* (Valley Forge: Judson Press, 1971).

Notes

[2]"Come Out de Wilderness" from *Songs of Zion,* Supplemental Worship Resources 12 (Nashville: Abingdon Press, 1981), p. 136. The song is in the public domain.

[3]"He Looked Beyond My Fault" by Dottie Rambo. Copyright © 1968 by John T. Benson Publishing Company/ASCAP. All rights reserved. Used by permission of the Benson Company, Inc.

[4]Preston Robert Washington, *From the Pew to the Pavement* (Morristown, N.J.: Aaron Press, 1986).

[5]Warren H. Stewart, Sr., *Interpreting God's Word in Black Preaching* (Valley Forge: Judson Press, 1984). An excellent resource for black preachers in search of hermeneutical methods that might sharpen their sermon preparation and delivery.

Chapter 5

[1]See "Statistics on Harlem," February 18, 1988, draft edition, Harlem Urban Development Corporation, A.C. Powell State Office Building, 125th St. and A.C. Powell Blvd., 17th floor, New York, NY 10027.

[2]*The New York Times,* August 1, 1983.

[3]See Elliott D. Lee's article "Churches Building Heaven on Earth," *Black Enterprise* magazine, August 1981. Memorial is listed in this article as a congregation involved in housing ministry and economic recovery of the community.

[4]Wallace Charles Smith, *The Church in the Life of the Black Family* (Valley Forge: Judson Press, 1985).

[5]It should be noted that it takes an applicant to the New York Housing Authority eighteen years to receive an apartment. See Jonathan Kozol, "The Homeless and Their Children," parts 1 and 2, *The New Yorker,* (1/25 and 2/1/88).

[6]Preston Robert Washington, "Who Must Develop Harlem?" *New York Amsterdam News,* 6/6/87.

Appendix

[1]Dietrich Bonhoeffer, *The Cost of Discipleship* (New York: Macmillan Publishing Co., 1963), p. 47.

[2]*Ibid.,* p. 48.

[3]Jeffrey D. Jones, *Vision for Leadership*

[4]*Ibid.,* p. 3.

[5]*Ibid.*

[6]John William Zehring, *Making Your Life Count* (Valley Forge: Judson Press, 1980), p. 26.

[7]Dan Otto Via, Jr., *The Parables* (Philadelphia: Fortress Press, 1967), p. 115.

[8]*Ibid.*

[9]*Ibid.*

[10]Zehring, *Making,* p. 26.

[11]Martin Luther King, Jr., *Strength to Love* (Philadelphia: Fortress Press, 1981), pp. 17, 19.

[12]*Ibid.,* p. 20.